SIMPLE

THE EASIEST
COOKBOOK
IN THE WORLD

NO RECIPE HAS MORE THAN
4 STEPS OR 6 INGREDIENTS

JEAN-FRANÇOIS MALLET

BLACK DOG
& LEVENTHAL
PUBLISHERS
NEW YORK

This book, the result of years of experience, comes as an answer to the question I ask myself almost every day: "What on earth can I cook this evening?" It can be a real challenge to come up with ideas for everyday cuisine—for children and adults—and to create new dishes with the few ingredients in your refrigerator or cupboard.

This book is my attempt to share some everyday quick and easy recipes for all tastes. Once you know how to combine flavors and basic ingredients it's quite possible to make tasty dishes—and even impress people—without spending hours cooking.

This book is surprisingly simple: 2 to 6 ingredients are shown in photographs with a few lines of text. All you have to do is cook . . . and presto, it's ready!

I hope you enjoy the recipes, and, especially, the results!

TABLE OF CONTENTS

INSTRUCTIONS

For these recipes you need the following:

- Running water
- An oven
- A refrigerator
- A skillet
- A large cast-iron saucepan
- A sharp knife
- Salt and pepper
- Oil: extra virgin is always the best, but also hazelnut, sesame, and walnut

(If you don't possess these, now is the time to invest!)

What ingredients are indispensable?

- **Canned food:** tuna and sardines in oil, coconut milk, gazpacho, and the essential trio of canned tomato products (chopped tomatoes, tomato paste, and crushed tomatoes/tomato purée)
- **Crème fraîche:** cream fermented with a bacterial culture, like yogurt. It is slightly sweeter and has a higher fat content than products labeled "sour cream," although sour cream does make a good direct substitute if crème fraîche is unavailable.
- **Herbs:** Nothing beats fresh herbs. You must use fresh herbs! If you are out, you can always use frozen or dried versions (but they are not as good).
- **Oils:** Olive oil—extra virgin is always the best; also hazelnut, sesame, and walnut.
- **Pasta:** Vary the type of pasta suggested in the recipes depending on your tastes (and what you have in the cupboard).
- **Preserved lemon:** sliced or whole lemon fermented in a pickling brine including their own juice, sometimes with added spices. The peel is used to flavor dishes from North Africa and South Asia. Fresh lemon zest with a pinch of salt makes an adequate substitute if preserved lemon isn't available.
- **Soy sauce:** Preferably Japanese, the Kikkoman® variety with the green top—it's less salty.

What method?

- **Boiling pasta:** Boil it in a large saucepan full of lightly salted water. Keep an eye on the cooking time if you like your pasta *al dente*.
- **Cooking in a bain-marie:** This technique allows you to melt or cook food without burning it. Place the bowl, baking dish, or saucepan containing the preparation into another larger container partially filled with boiling water.
- **Marinating:** Soaking an ingredient in an aromatic preparation to make it more flavorsome or tender
- **Beating the egg whites into peaks:** Add a pinch of salt and use an electric mixer,

gradually increasing the speed. So you don't break the egg whites, always beat them in the same direction.

• **Whipping cream:** To do this successfully the cream and bowl must be very cold (put the bowl in the freezer for a few minutes). Use an electric mixer.

• **Peeling an orange:** Cut off the two ends of the orange. With a knife, gradually draw back the peel and white membrane, while slipping the blade between the peel and the fruit working from top to bottom.

• **Reducing:** Reducing the level of a juice or a broth on the stove by evaporation (so without the lid on) while it simmers. This process produces more concentrated flavors.

• **Peeling the outer skin of a lemon:** There are three ways of doing this: For novices and to obtain very fine slivers of zest, use a cheese grater with just one stroke each time, without going as deep as the pith. To obtain zest that looks like vermicelli use a lemon zester. To obtain shavings or a coarse grated effect use a vegetable peeler.

• **Greasing a pan for baking:** coating a pan with a thin layer of fat so that baked items will not stick to it. Use a clean paper towel to spread a tablespoon of butter or a flavorless oil over the top surface.

Which kitchen utensil?

• **Electric mixer:** With its blades, it's perfect for mixing sauces, beating egg whites, or whipping cream. Of course, you can use a non-electric beater and some elbow grease, as well!

• **Hand (immersion) blender:** used for liquid preparations (soups, smoothies, milkshakes). It is handy, practical, and inexpensive. What's more, it means fewer dishes to wash because you use it directly in the preparation, without the need to pour it into another bowl.

• **Blender:** More expensive and cumbersome than the hand blender, but it provides a creamier, more velvety texture. However, it means more dishes to wash.

• **Food processor:** As its name indicates, this is a multi-purpose tool. It has various accessories, such as a blade, beater, slicer, mincer, and emulsifier.

What oven settings?

200°F/90°C: 3	300°F/150°C: 5	400°F/210°C: 7	500°F/270°C: 9
250°F/120°C: 4	350°F/180°C: 6	450°F/240°C: 8	575°F/300°C: 10

That's it.
Now all you have to do is follow the recipe!

THE RECIPES

CHEESE PUFFS

Puff pastry
x 1 sheet

Grated Provolone or Parmesan cheese
7 ounces (200 g)

Preparation time: 5 min., plus 25 min. freezing time
Cooking time: 25 min.

- On parchment paper, unroll the **puff pastry** and sprinkle the **cheese** over the entire surface. Using the parchment as a guide, tightly roll up the pastry. Freeze for 20 minutes.
- Preheat the oven to 350°F/180°C.
- Remove the dough from the freezer. Cut the pastry into ¼-inch-thick (½ cm) slices and place them on a baking sheet. Bake for 25 minutes. Enjoy as a warm appetizer.

PARMESAN AND OLIVE SHORTBREADS

Black olives
x 20 (pitted)

Parmesan cheese
5 ounces (150 g)

Softened butter
½ cup (1 stick; 110 g)

Flour
¾ cup (100 g)

**Preparation time:
25 min.
Chilling time: 1 hr.
Cooking time: 15 min.**

- Chop the olives and grate the **Parmesan**. On a clean work surface, knead together the **olives**, **Parmesan**, **butter**, and **flour**. Shape into a log and refrigerate for 1 hour.
- Preheat the oven to 350°F/180°C.
- Remove the dough from the refrigerator, and cut it into ½-inch-thick (1 cm) slices. Place them on a baking sheet and bake for 15 minutes.
- Remove from the oven. Cool before removing them from the sheet.

SAUSAGE, ROSEMARY, AND LEMON MINI PIZZAS

Rosemary
1 sprig

Pizza dough
1 ball (6 ounces/170 g; thawed if frozen)

Pork sausage link
7 ounces (200 g)

Lemon
x 1

Preparation time: 15 min.
Cooking time: 25 min.

- Preheat the oven to 325°F/170°C.
- Strip the leaves off the **rosemary** and chop them. Zest the **lemon**.
- Roll out the **pizza dough** into a 2-inch (5 cm) circle and cut out 12 small rounds with a biscuit cutter or round glass.
- Cut the **sausage** crosswise into 12 equal slices. Place 1 slice of sausage on each piece of dough. Place them all on a baking sheet.
- Bake for 25 minutes. Remove from the oven. Sprinkle with the **rosemary** and **lemon** zest before serving.

PARMESAN CHORIZO MUFFINS

Flour
1 cup plus 2 tablespoons (150 g)

Baking powder
2 teaspoons (10 g)

Eggs
x 3

Milk
½ cup (120 mL)

Grated Parmesan cheese
3½ ounces (100 g)

Chorizo
4½ ounces (130 g)

drizzle extra-virgin olive oil

🚹🚹🚹🚹

🕐

Preparation time: 15 min.
Cooking time: 25 min.

• Preheat the oven to 350°F/180°C. Mix the **flour** and **baking powder**. Add the **eggs** and **milk**. Finely dice the **chorizo** and mix together with the **Parmesan**. Add the cheese mixture to the egg mixture. Fill eight small lightly oiled muffin molds or four large ones with the mixture. Bake for 25 minutes. Enjoy hot or cold with salad, if desired.

WHIPPED CREAM WITH SMOKED SALMON

Smoked salmon
6 slices

Dill
1 bunch

Heavy (whipping) cream
11 fluid ounces (330 mL)

Organic lemons
x 2

**Preparation time:
10 min.**

- Dice the **salmon**. Wash and chop the **dill**. Zest and juice the **lemons**, straining out any seeds.
- With an electric mixer, whip the **cream** in a cold bowl until it holds soft peaks.
- Stir in the **salmon**, **dill**, **lemon zest**, and **juice**.
- Transfer to a serving dish.

RICOTTA AND GREEN PEA SPREAD

Organic lemons
x 2

Green peas
1 cup (130 g), fresh or frozen

Ricotta
1 cup (250 g)

Extra-virgin olive oil
¼ cup (60 mL)

Dried oregano
1 tablespoon (5 g)

Toast

 Salt, pepper

**Preparation time:
10 min.**

- Zest and juice the **lemons**, straining out any seeds.
- Boil the **peas** for 2 minutes and then drain.
- Mix the peas with the **ricotta**, **olive oil**, **oregano**, **lemon zest**, and **juice**.
- Season with salt and pepper and enjoy on slices of **toast**.

CELERY WITH SMOKED SALMON

Celery
4 (small) ribs

Smoked salmon
4 slices

Plain yogurt
1 cup (250 g)

Curry powder
1 tablespoon (5 g)

Extra-virgin olive oil
1 tablespoon (15 mL)

 **Salt, pepper**

♣♣♣♣

**Preparation time:
10 min.**

- Slice the **celery** lengthwise into small even strips, with or without their leaves. Wrap each strip with a piece of **smoked salmon**.
- Blend the **yogurt**, **curry powder**, and **olive oil** to make a dip.
- Season with salt and pepper. Dip the **celery** into the sauce, and enjoy.

12

STUFFED APRICOTS

Apricots (firm)
x 16

Blood sausage links
7 ounces (200 g)

**Preparation time:
15 min.
Cooking time: 25 min.**

- Preheat the oven to 350°F/180°C.
- Split the **apricots** and remove the pits.
- Remove the casing from the **sausage** and crush the meat with a fork.
- Stuff 16 **apricots halves** with the **sausage**, and cover them with the remaining 16 halves. Place them in a baking dish and bake for 25 minutes. Enjoy piping hot.

ROASTED ASPARAGUS WITH PROSCIUTTO

Green asparagus spears
x 20

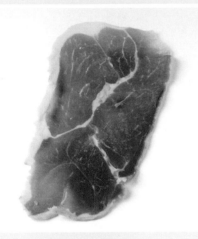

Prosciutto
10 slices

Preparation time: 15 min.
Cooking time: 10 min.

- Preheat the oven to 350°F/180°C.
- Remove the tough woody ends from the **asparagus**. Cut each **prosciutto** slice into 2 pieces.
- Wrap each **asparagus** spear with 1 piece of **prosciutto**. Place them on a baking sheet. Bake for 10 minutes.
- Enjoy warm with mayonnaise, if desired.

HUMMUS WITH CUMIN

Chickpeas
1 can (530 g drained)

Extra-virgin olive oil
6 tablespoons (90 mL)

Garlic
2 cloves

Lemon
x 1

Cumin seeds
2 tablespoons (20 g)

**Preparation time:
10 min.**

• Drain and rinse the **chickpeas**. Place in a saucepan with 3½ tablespoons water and heat. Chop the **garlic** and juice the **lemon**. Transfer the chickpeas and their cooking water to a blender and add 5 tablespoons of **olive oil**, the garlic, lemon juice, and half the **cumin seeds**. Blend until smooth.

• Season with salt and pepper and allow to cool. Spread on a serving platter and drizzle with the remaining 1 tablespoon oil and cumin seeds.

TUNA SASHIMI WITH WATERMELON

Soy sauce
3 tablespoons (45 mL)

Extra-virgin olive oil
3 tablespoons (45 mL)

Tuna or bonito
1⅓ pounds (600 g), red or white

Watermelon
1⅓ pounds (600 g; 1 large slice)

**Preparation time:
10 min.**

- Mix the **soy sauce** with the **olive oil**.
- Cut the **tuna** into small thick pieces, ¾ inch (2 cm) square.
- Remove the rind from the **watermelon** and cut it into pieces similar in size to the **tuna**.
- Arrange equal amounts of the **tuna** and **watermelon** on 4 plates, alternating them. Refrigerate until ready to serve.
- Coat with sauce 2 minutes before serving.

SHIRRED EGGS WITH SMOKED SALMON

Smoked salmon
2 slices

Eggs
x 4

Heavy cream
¾ cup (180 mL)

Butter
3½ tablespoons (50 g)

 **Salt, pepper**

👤👤👤👤

🕐

Preparation time: 5 min.
Cooking time:
10 to 12 min.

• Preheat the oven to 325°F/170°C. Coat four small ramekins with the **butter**. Cut the **salmon** into pieces and divide half of it evenly among the ramekins. Add 1 **egg** and 3 tablespoons (45 mL) of the **cream** to each ramekin. Season with salt and pepper. Bake for 10 to 12 minutes in a bain-marie. Distribute the remaining salmon on top and enjoy.

QUICHE LORRAINE

Eggs
x 4

Heavy cream
¾ cup (360 mL)

Grated Swiss cheese
7 ounces (200 g)

Puff pastry
x 1 sheet

Ham
9 ounces (255 g)

Salt, pepper

**Preparation time:
15 min.
Cooking time: 45 min.**

• Preheat the oven to 350°F/180°C. Beat the **eggs** with the **cream** and **cheese**. Season with salt and pepper. Place the **pastry** in a pie pan, turning down and flattening the edges. Pour the egg mixture into the pastry. Cut the **ham** into small pieces and distribute them evenly over the egg mixture. Bake for 45 minutes. Enjoy.

CHERRIES WITH BACON

Bacon
10 thin slices

Cherries
x 20

Preparation time: 5 min.
Cooking time: 10 min.

- Preheat the oven to 350°F/180°C. Cut the **bacon** slices in half widthwise.
- Wash, dry, and pit the **cherries**. Wrap each one with a **bacon** slice and place on a baking sheet. Bake for 10 minutes.
- Enjoy warm as an appetizer.

PROSCIUTTO PALMIERS

Puff pastry
x 1 sheet

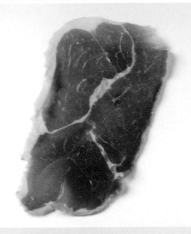

Prosciutto
7 ounces (200 g), thinly sliced

**Preparation time:
10 min., plus 20 min.
freezing time
Cooking time: 25 min.**

• Preheat the oven to 375°F/200°C. Unroll the **puff pastry** without removing the parchment paper. Cover the whole surface of the pastry with the **prosciutto**. Roll up the pastry, starting at one short end and using the parchment to keep the roll tight, and freeze for 20 minutes. Use the same parchment paper to line a baking sheet. Cut the pastry roll crosswise into ¼-inch-thick (½ cm) slices and set them on the baking sheet. Bake for 25 minutes until nicely browned. Enjoy as an appetizer.

FRENCH ONION SOUP

Mild onions
x 4

Butter
1½ tablespoons (20 g)

Extra-virgin olive oil
¼ cup (120 mL)

Chicken broth
1 quart (1 L)

Baguette
20 slices

Grated cheese
4¼ ounces (120 g)

**Preparation time:
10 min.
Cooking time: 45 min.**

- Peel and thinly slice the **onions**. Heat the **butter** and **olive oil** in a heavy-based casserole dish. Add the onions and stew for 20 minutes. Add the **chicken broth** and cook for 10 minutes more. Preheat the broiler.
- Pour out the soup into four oven-safe bowls. Top each with 5 **baguette slices** and one-quarter of the **cheese**. Broil for 15 minutes, until nicely browned.

GAZPACHO WITH ASPARAGUS

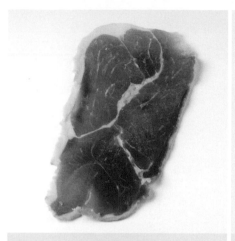

Prosciutto
4 slices

Green asparagus
x 8

White asparagus
2 large jars
(12 ounces or 330 g each)

Extra-virgin olive oil
2 tablespoons (30 mL)

**Preparation time:
10 min.
Cooking time: 15 min.**

- Preheat the oven to 350°F/180°C. Wash the **green asparagus** and remove the tough woody ends.
- Arrange the slices of **prosciutto** and **green asparagus** on a baking sheet. Bake for 10 minutes. Remove from the oven and cool slightly, then cut everything into small pieces.
- In a saucepan, bring the **white asparagus** and the water from their jars just to a boil, drain, and then purée the stalks in a blender.
- Equally divide the **white asparagus purée** among 4 plates. Top with the **green asparagus** and **prosciutto**. Drizzle with **olive oil** and serve.

CREAM OF CELERIAC WITH SALMON ROE

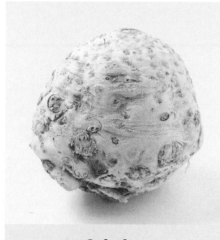

Celeriac
x 1 (1 pound or 455 g)

Light cream
3 tablespoons (45 g)

SALMON ROE
2 tablespoons (30 g)

Extra-virgin olive oil
2 tablespoons (30 mL)

 Salt, pepper

**Preparation time:
20 min.
Cooking time: 45 min.**

• Peel and dice the **celeriac** and place it in a saucepan with enough lightly salted water to cover. Boil over high heat for 35 minutes.

• Drain the water and return the celeriac to the pot. Add the **light cream** and simmer over medium heat for an additional 10 minutes. Season with salt and pepper and mix everything together. Remove from the heat and cool.

• Evenly divide the **celeriac** mixture among 4 small cups, top each with **salmon roe**, add a drizzle of **olive oil**, and enjoy.

CREAMED PEAS WITH CRAB

Basil
1 bunch

Green peas
1¼ cups (400 g) (fresh or frozen)

Cream
4 teaspoons (50 mL)

Snow crab meat
1 can (6 oz., 170 g)

 Salt, pepper

👤👤👤👤

🕐

**Preparation time:
10 min.
Cooking time: 10 min.**

• Wash the **basil** and remove the leaves; pat dry. Bring 2 cups **water** to a boil, add the **peas**, and cook for 5 minutes. Add the **cream**, season with salt and pepper, and transfer to a blender. Add the basil and pulse until well combined.

• Allow to cool. Divide among four shallow bowls. Top with the **crab meat** and enjoy.

CREAM OF CAULIFLOWER WITH SESAME OIL

Cauliflower
x 1 (1 pound or 455 g)

Light cream
5 tablespoons (75 g)

Sesame seeds
2 tablespoons (15 g)

Sesame oil
¼ cup (60 mL)

 Salt, pepper

**Preparation time:
15 min.
Cooking time: 40 min.**

• Cut the **cauliflower** into small pieces and place in a saucepan with enough water to cover. Simmer for 40 minutes over low heat.

• Using a hand blender, blend the **cauliflower** with the cooking water, adding the **light cream** and seasoning with salt and pepper.

• Divide among 4 individual bowls, sprinkle with **sesame seeds**, add a drizzle of **sesame oil**, and enjoy.

ZUCCHINI GAZPACHO WITH BASIL

Basil
1 bunch

Zucchini
x 4

Pesto
1 tablespoon (15 g)

Extra-virgin olive oil
6 tablespoons (90 mL)

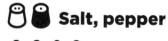 **Salt, pepper**

👥👥👥👥

🕐

**Preparation time:
10 min.
Cooking time: 30 min.**

- Wash the **basil** and remove the leaves.
- Wash and roughly chop the **zucchini** and place it into a saucepan with 1 cup (240 mL) of water and boil for 30 minutes.
- Add the **pesto**, **olive oil**, and three-fourths of the **basil** leaves. Mix with a hand blender. Season with salt and pepper. Cool. Stir in the remaining **basil** and serve.

TOMATO GAZPACHO WITH RED BELL PEPPERS

Red bell peppers
x 2

Cucumber
x 1

Extra-virgin olive oil
6 tablespoons (90 mL)

Crushed tomatoes
1 can (28 ounces or 800 g)

Vinegar
¼ cup (60 mL)

Cherry tomatoes
7 ounces (200 g)

 **Salt, pepper**

👤👤👤👤

🕐

**Preparation time:
10 min.
Cooking time: 5 min.**

• Stem and seed the **red bell peppers**. Place them in a saucepan filled with boiling water. Remove them after 5 minutes.

• Peel and seed the **cucumber** and cut it into cubes. In a blender, mix together all of the ingredients, except the **cherry tomatoes**.

• Cut the **cherry tomatoes** in half and stir them into the **red bell pepper** mixture. Season with salt and pepper and enjoy.

CREAM OF WINTER SQUASH WITH HAZELNUTS

Hazelnuts
x 20

Winter squash
x 1 (1¾ pounds or 800 g)

Light cream
7 ounces (200 g)

Hazelnut oil
¼ cup (60 mL), plus extra
for drizzling

Salt, pepper

Preparation time:
10 min.
Cooking time: 40 min.

- Crush the **hazelnuts**.
- Peel the **winter squash** and cut it into large cubes. Place in a saucepan with enough water to cover. Boil for 35 minutes.
- Add the **cream** and **hazelnut oil**. Return to a boil. Remove from the heat and blend with a hand blender. Season with salt and pepper. Garnish with the **hazelnuts** and a drizzle of **hazelnut oil**.

SALMON SATAY NOODLE BOWL

Broccoli crowns
9 ounces (255 g)

Rice vermicelli
2½ ounces (70 g)

Chicken broth cubes
½ cube

Satay sauce
2 tablespoons (30 mL)

Salmon fillets
1½ pounds (680 g), boneless, skinless

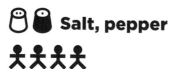 **Salt, pepper**

**Preparation time:
10 min.
Cooking time: 7 min.**

- Cut the **broccoli** into small pieces.
- In a large saucepan, combine all the ingredients, except the **salmon**, with 5 cups (1.2 liters) of water. Cook for 5 minutes over low heat while stirring.
- Cut the **salmon** into cubes and add them to the saucepan. Cook for 2 minutes more.
- Divide among 4 large bowls, season with salt and pepper, and enjoy piping hot.

COCONUT CURRY NOODLE BOWL WITH SHRIMP

Thai basil
20 leaves

Raw shrimp
x 20

Rice vermicelli
3 ounces (85 g)

Chicken broth cube
½ cube

Curry powder
2 tablespoons (10 g)

Coconut milk
32 fluid ounces (1 L)

 **Salt, pepper**

👤👤👤👤

🕐

**Preparation time:
10 min.
Cooking time: 20 min.
Standing time: 5 min.**

- Wash the **basil** leaves and chop them. Shell the **shrimp**.
- In a large saucepan, combine all the ingredients, except the **basil** and **rice vermicelli**, with 2½ cups (600 mL) of water. Simmer on low heat for 15 minutes.
- Stir in the **basil** and **rice vermicelli**. Turn off the heat, cover, and let stand for 5 minutes. Stir to mix. Season with salt and pepper and serve.

CHICKEN AND ZUCCHINI SOUP

Basil
20 leaves

Zucchini
x 2

Scallions
x 2

Chicken breasts
x 4, boneless, skinless

Chicken broth cube
½ cube

 Salt, pepper

**Preparation time:
10 min.
Cooking time: 20 min.
Standing time: 5 min.**

• Wash the **basil** leaves and chop them. After removing the ends, thinly slice the **zucchini** and **scallions**. Cut the **chicken** into bite-size pieces.

• In large saucepan, combine all the ingredients, except the **basil**, with 5 cups (1.2 liters) of water. Cook for 20 minutes over low heat.

• Add the **basil**. Cover, remove from the heat, and let stand 5 minutes. Season with salt and pepper, mix, and enjoy.

BROTH WITH BEEF AND MUSTARD

Cherry tomatoes
x 20

Freshly ground beef
10 ounces (300 g)

Chicken broth cube
½ cube

Dijon mustard
1 tablespoon (10 g)

Fresh thyme leaves
2 tablespoons (5 g)

Pasta shells
3 ounces (85 g)

 **Salt, pepper**

**Preparation time:
10 min.
Cooking time: 20 min.
Standing time: 5 min.**

- Wash the **cherry tomatoes** and cut them in half. Form the **beef** into small 1-inch (3 cm) balls.
- In a large saucepan, combine all the ingredients, except the **meatballs**, with 5 cups (1.2 liters) of water. Cook for 20 minutes on high heat, stirring occasionally. Add meatballs during the last ten minutes.
- Skim off any foam, cover, and let stand for 5 minutes. Season with salt and pepper, stir, and enjoy.

GOAT CHEESE TOAST SALAD

Green asparagus
x 20

Green beans
14 ounces (400 g)

Small rounds goat's milk cheese
x 4

Baguette
8 slices

Honey
2 tablespoons (40 g)

Cider vinegar
2 tablespoons (30 mL)

 Salt, pepper

Preparation time: 15 min.
Cooking time: 15 min.

- Preheat the oven to 350°F/180°C. Wash the **asparagus** and **green beans**. Remove the tough woody ends from the **asparagus** and trim the **green beans**. Boil the vegetables for 5 minutes in lightly salted water. Drain.
- Cut the **goat cheese rounds** in half widthwise, put 1 piece on each **baguette** slice, and place them on a baking sheet. Drizzle with **honey**. Bake for 10 minutes.
- Divide the **asparagus** and **green beans** among 4 plates. Place 2 hot toasts on each plate, season with **vinegar**, salt, and pepper, and enjoy.

ASPARAGUS, PARMESAN, AND SOFT-BOILED EGGS

Green asparagus
x 20

Extra-virgin olive oil
¼ cup (60 mL)

Oranges
x 2

Eggs
x 4

Roughly grated Parmesan cheese
2 cups (160 g)

 Salt, pepper

⏱

Preparation time: 15 min.
Cooking time: 10 min.

- Zest and juice the **oranges**, straining out any seeds. Wash the **asparagus** and remove the tough woody ends.
- Boil the **asparagus** for 5 minutes in lightly salted water. Drain. Return to the pot and add the **olive oil** and **orange** zest and juice.
- Boil the **eggs** for exactly 5 minutes. Cool, peel, and cut in half.
- Arrange the **asparagus** and **oranges** on a serving platter and top with the **eggs**. Sprinkle on the **Parmesan** and season with salt and pepper.

WHITE BEAN PESTO SALAD

White beans, canned, rinsed
x 3 (8 ounce, 225 g)

Red onions
x 2 (small)

Pesto
2 tablespoons (30 g)

Extra-virgin olive oil
¼ cup (60 mL)

Light cream
2 tablespoons (30 mL)

Basil
8 leaves

 Salt, pepper

**Preparation time:
10 min.
Cooking time: 30 min.**

- Shell the **beans** and boil them for 30 minutes. Cool in their cooking water.
- Peel and thinly slice the **onions**.
- Drain the **beans** and return them to the pot. Mix in the **pesto**, **onions**, **olive oil**, **cream**, and **basil**. Season with salt and pepper and enjoy.

MELON WITH SMOKED SALMON AND MINT

Melon
x 1

Smoked salmon
4 slices

Mint
4 sprigs

Extra-virgin olive oil
6 tablespoons (90 mL)

Lime
½

 **Salt, pepper**

👤👤👤👤

**Preparation time:
10 min.
Standing time: 2 minutes**

- Cut the **melon** into cubes. Dice the **salmon**. Wash the **mint**, remove the leaves, and finely chop them.
- Combine the **melon**, **salmon**, and **mint**.
- Add the **olive oil**. Squeeze the **lime** juice over. Season with salt and pepper. Mix, let stand for 2 minutes, and enjoy.

MELON, TOMATO, AND BASIL SALAD

Melon
x1

Cherry tomatoes
x20

Extra-virgin olive oil
¼ cup (60 mL)

Basil
20 leaves

Dried oregano
1 teaspoon

 **Salt, pepper**

👤👤👤👤

🕑

Preparation time: 5 min.

- Cut the **melon** into cubes and the **tomatoes** in half.
- Combine the **melon** and **tomatoes** with the **olive oil**, **basil** leaves, and **oregano**. Season with salt and pepper and enjoy.

AVOCADOS WITH SMOKED SALMON

Smoked salmon
4 thick slices

Dill
4 sprigs

Limes
x 2

Extra-virgin olive oil
¼ cup (60 mL)

Avocados
x 4 (ripe)

Chives
1 bunch

Salt, pepper

**Preparation time:
10 min.**

- Cut the **salmon** into small cubes. Finely chop the **chives**. Juice the **limes**.
- In a bowl, mix the **salmon** with the **chives**, **lime** juice, and **olive oil**. Season with salt and pepper.
- Split the **avocados** and remove the pit. Fill them with the **smoked salmon**. Season with salt and pepper. Chop the dill, sprinkle over, and enjoy immediately.

LENTIL SALAD WITH SALMON AND TARRAGON

Green lentils
7 ounces (200 g)

Salmon fillets
2 (7 ounces or 200 g each), skinless

Tarragon
8 sprigs

Full-grain mustard
1 tablespoon (10 g)

Extra-virgin olive oil
¼ cup (60 mL)

 Salt, pepper

Preparation time: 5 min.
Cooking time: 25 min.

• Boil the **lentils** in plenty of water for 20 minutes. Add the **salmon** and cook for 5 minutes more without stirring. Strain everything and cool.

• Wash and chop the **tarragon**. Cut the **salmon** into bite-size pieces and mix it back into the **lentils**. Stir in the **tarragon** and remaining ingredients. Season with salt and pepper and serve.

SALMON TABBOULEH WITH RADISHES

Radishes
x 8

Mint
20 leaves

Lemons
x 2 (or ¼ cup [60 mL]
fresh lemon juice)

Salmon fillets
x 2 (7 ounces or 200 g each),
skinless

**Fine-grain couscous,
uncooked**
¼ cup (45 g)

Extra-virgin olive oil
¼ cup (60 mL)

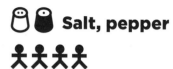 **Salt, pepper**

🏃🏃🏃🏃

⏱

**Preparation time:
10 min.
Cooking time: 25 min.**

• Wash and thinly slice the **radishes**. Wash the **mint** leaves and finely chop them. Juice the **lemons**, straining out any seeds. Cut the **salmon** into small cubes.

• In a bowl, mix the **couscous**, **radishes**, **salmon**, **mint**, **lemon juice**, and **olive oil**, Season with salt and pepper. Refrigerate for 25 minutes and enjoy cold.

CAESAR SALAD WITH SHRIMP

Romaine lettuce
x 1

Sour cream
2 tablespoons (30 mL)

Cooked jumbo shrimp
x 16

Extra-virgin olive oil
¼ cup (60 mL)

Chopped Parmesan cheese
¼ cup (20 g)

Crisp bread
4 slices

🧂🧂 **Salt, pepper**

🚶🚶🚶🚶

🕑
Preparation time:
10 min.

• Separate and rinse the **lettuce** leaves. Put them in a salad bowl and toss with the **sour cream**, **shrimp**, **olive oil**, and **cheese**. Season with salt and pepper. Break the **bread** into pieces, add them to the salad, toss again, and enjoy.

• Don't have any shrimp? Swap in 2 grilled chicken breasts, chopped in bite-sized pieces.

VERY GREEN SALAD

Green beans
7 ounces (200 g)

Zucchini
x 2

Green peas
7 ounces (200 g), fresh or frozen

Baby gem lettuce
x 2

Mint
20 leaves

Chives
1 bunch

Salt, pepper

4 tablespoons extra-virgin olive oil

Preparation time: 15 min.
Cooking time: 20 min.

• Bring a saucepan of lightly salted water to a boil. Slice the **zucchini**. Add the zucchini, **green beans**, and **peas** to the boiling water and cook for 2 to 3 minutes. Drain and cool under cold running water.

• Mix the vegetables with the **lettuce**. Cut the **herbs** over the salad with scissors and toss to combine. Drizzle with **olive oil**, season with salt and pepper, and enjoy.

THAI SALAD

Cilantro
1 bunch

Beef carpaccio
14 ounces (400 g),
approximately 4 portions

Sesame seeds
2 tablespoons (16 g)

Limes
x 2

Soy sauce
¼ cup (60 mL)

Green chile
x 1 (small)

+ pan with oil

**Preparation time:
10 min.
Cooking time: 1 min.**

- Wash and chop the **cilantro**. Juice the **limes**. Chop the **green chile**.
- In a skillet over high heat, sauté the **beef** with the **olive oil** for 1 minute. Turn off the heat and cool.
- Add the **sesame seeds**, **lime** juice, **cilantro**, **soy sauce**, and **green chile**. Mix and enjoy with rice, if desired.

SALAD WITH ROQUEFORT CHEESE

Shallots
x 4 (large)

Flour
¾ cup (90 g)

Little Gem lettuce
x 4

Roquefort cheese
1 cup (130 g)

Walnut oil
½ cup (120 mL)

Cider vinegar
¼ cup (60 mL)

**Salt, pepper
+ sauté pan with 2 inches
(5 cm) of frying oil**

**Preparation time:
20 min.
Cooking time: 5 min.**

• Peel and thinly slice the **shallots**. Dredge them in the **flour**. Heat the frying oil in the skillet to 350°F/180°C.

• Add the **shallots** and fry for 5 minutes, or until golden brown. Remove and set aside.

• Quarter the **lettuces**; cut the **Roquefort** into small pieces. Add them to a salad bowl and mix with the **walnut oil** and **vinegar**. Season with salt and pepper. Top with the fried shallots and serve.

• For a heartier salad, toss with 7 ounces (200 g) thinly sliced, cooked flank steak.

BOW TIE PASTA WITH BROCCOLI, RADICCHIO, AND HAZELNUTS

Broccoli crowns
4 ounces (115 g)

Radicchio
5 ounces (140 g)

Hazelnuts
x 20

Extra-virgin olive oil
¼ cup (60 mL)

Bow tie pasta
10 ounces (300 g)

Parmesan cheese wedge
3½ ounces (100 g)

 Salt, pepper

☺☺☺☺

🕐

**Preparation time:
15 min.
Cooking time: 20 min.**

- Cut the **broccoli** into pieces; thinly slice the **radicchio**; grind the **hazelnuts**; grate the **Parmesan**.
- In a large skillet over low heat, sauté the **broccoli** in the **olive oil**. Cook for 10 minutes.
- Boil the **bow tie pasta** for 11 minutes, just to *al dente*, in lightly salted water. Drain and reserve 1 tablespoon (15 mL) of cooking liquid. Add the drained pasta and reserved cooking liquid to the skillet. Sprinkle with the **Parmesan**. Season with salt and pepper and heat through for 5 minutes.

ROAST BEEF SALAD WITH BASIL

Basil
1 bunch

Cucumber
¼

Roast beef
14 ounces (400 g)

Extra-virgin olive oil
¼ cup (60 mL)

Soy sauce
1 tablespoon (15 mL)

 Salt, pepper

👨👨👨👨

🕐

**Preparation time:
15 min.
Cooking time: 5 min.**

- Wash the **basil** and remove the leaves. Thinly slice the **cucumber**.
- In a large bowl, combine the **roast beef**, **cucumber**, and **basil**.
- Add the **olive oil** and **soy sauce**. Season with salt and pepper and enjoy.

BOW TIE PASTA WITH GREEN VEGETABLES

Zucchini
x 1

Green asparagus
x 10

Green peas
7 ounces (200 g), fresh or frozen

Extra-virgin olive oil
¼ cup (60 mL)

Bow tie pasta
10 ounces (300 g)

Chives
1 bunch

 **Salt, pepper**

👤👤👤👤

🕐

**Preparation time:
15 min.
Cooking time: 20 min.**

- Snip the **chives** and set aside. Slice the **zucchini**. Wash and peel the **asparagus**, and cut it into pieces. Place the **zucchini**, **asparagus**, **peas**, and **olive oil** in a large skillet. Sauté over medium-high heat for 10 minutes.
- Boil the **bow tie pasta** for 11 minutes, just to *al dente*, in lightly salted water. Drain and reserve 1 tablespoon (15 mL) of cooking liquid. Add the drained pasta and reserved cooking liquid to the skillet, along with the **chives**. Heat for 5 minutes. Sprinkle with Parmesan if desired, season with salt and pepper, and serve.

FUSILLI WITH SARDINES

Mandarin oranges
x 2

Pine nuts
¼ cup (35 g)

Fusilli
10 ounces (300 g)

Sardines in olive oil
x 2 cans (4.5 ounces or 125 g each)

Raisins
¼ cup (35 g)

 Salt, pepper

**Preparation time:
10 min.
Cooking time: 15 min.**

- Peel the **mandarin oranges** and cut into small pieces.
- In a dry skillet over medium heat, toast the **pine nuts** until golden, about 3 minutes. Transfer to a bowl and set aside.
- Boil the **pasta** for 9 to 11 minutes, just to *al dente*, in lightly salted water. Drain and reserve 2 tablespoons (30 mL) of cooking liquid. Add the drained pasta and reserved cooking liquid to the skillet, along with the **sardines** in their oil, the **raisins**, and the **mandarin oranges**. Heat through, about 3 minutes, stirring. Season with salt and pepper. Sprinkle with **pine nuts** before serving.

MACARONI GRATIN

Macaroni
10 ounces (300 g)

Ham heel
9 ounces (255 g)

Grated Parmesan cheese
5 ounces (140 g)

Heavy cream
13 fluid ounces (390 mL)

Salt, pepper

Preparation time: 5 min.
Cooking time: 45 min.

• Preheat the oven to 350°F/180°C degrees.
• Boil the **macaroni** for 7 minutes, just to *al dente*, in lightly salted water. Drain and transfer to a gratin dish.
• Cut the **ham** into small pieces and add it to the **macaroni**, along with the **Parmesan**, **cream**, salt, and pepper. Stir to mix. Bake for 35 minutes. Once the gratin is golden brown, serve hot with a green salad, if desired.

RIGATONI ALL'ARRABBIATA WITH EGGPLANT

Eggplant
1 (long)

Extra-virgin olive oil
¼ cup (60 mL)

Chorizo
8 slices

Dried oregano
2 tablespoons (6 g)

Rigatoni
10 ounces (300 g)

 Salt, pepper

♁♁♁♁

⏱

**Preparation time:
10 min.
Cooking time: 30 min.**

• Cut the **eggplant** into pieces and sauté in a skillet with the **olive oil** over medium-high heat for 8 to 9 minutes. Add the **chorizo** and **oregano**. Continue cooking for 20 minutes while browning and stirring.

• Boil the **rigatoni** for 12 minutes, just to *al dente*, in lightly salted water. Drain and reserve 1 tablespoon (15 mL) of cooking water. Transfer the drained pasta and reserved cooking liquid to the skillet. Heat for 5 minutes, season with salt and pepper.

RIGATONI WITH DUCK

Duck
2 thighs

Button mushrooms
10 ounces (300 g)

Garlic
2 cloves

Rigatoni
10 ounces (300 g)

Chives
1 bunch

Grated Parmesan cheese
1 cup (100 g)

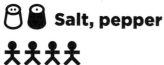 **Salt, pepper**

**Preparation time:
15 min.
Cooking time: 15 min.**

- Clean and thinly slice the **mushrooms**. Peel and chop the **garlic**. Finely chop the **chives**.
- Remove the **duck** meat and skin from the bones. Chop the meat and skin and place in a skillet over medium heat. Add the **mushrooms** and **garlic**. Cook for 10 minutes.
- Boil the **rigatoni** for 12 minutes, just to *al dente*, in lightly salted water. Drain and reserve 1 tablespoon (15 mL) of cooking water. Transfer the drained pasta and cooking liquid to the skillet. Add the **Parmesan** and **chives**. Cook for 2 minutes while stirring. Season with salt and pepper and serve.

PENNE WITH RED MULLET

Extra-virgin olive oil
¼ cup (60 mL)

Red onions
x 2

Red mullet fillets
x 4 (fresh or thawed frozen)

Dried oregano
1 tablespoon (5 g)

Penne
10 ounces (300 g)

 Salt, pepper

**Preparation time:
15 min.
Cooking time: 25 min.**

- Peel and thinly slice the **onions**.
- In a skillet over high heat, heat the **olive oil**. Add the **onions**. Sauté for 2 minutes, allowing them to brown. Add the **red mullet** and **oregano**. Cook for 10 minutes more, while stirring. Removed the mullet from the heat and cut into large pieces.
- Boil the **penne** for 11 minutes, just to *al dente*, in lightly salted water. Drain and reserve 2 tablespoons (30 mL) of cooking liquid. Transfer the drained penne and reserved cooking liquid to the skillet. Heat while stirring until the ingredients are uniformly warm. Season with salt and pepper.

PENNE WITH WINTER SQUASH AND WALNUTS

Winter squash
1 slice (approximately 14 ounces or 400 g)

Walnut oil
4 tablespoons (60 mL)

Penne
14 ounces (400 g)

Walnuts
x 10, shelled

Parmesan cheese wedge
3½ ounces (100 g)

 Salt, pepper

� � � �

🕒

Preparation time: 5 min.
Cooking time: 40 min.

- Preheat the oven to 350°F/180°C. Roast the **winter squash** with 2 tablespoons (30 mL) of **walnut oil** for 35 minutes.
- Boil the **penne** for 11 minutes, just to *al dente*, in lightly salted water.
- Roughly mash the **winter squash** with a fork. Chop the **walnuts**.
- In a skillet over medium-high heat, combine the **winter squash**, the remaining 2 tablespoons (30 mL) of **walnut oil**, the **penne**, and **walnuts**. Heat for 3 minutes. Season with salt and pepper. Sprinkle with grated **Parmesan** and enjoy.

90

PENNE WITH RED BELL PEPPERS AND BASIL

Red bell peppers
x 2

Garlic
4 cloves

Penne
10½ ounces (300 g)

Parmesan cheese wedge
3½ ounces (100 g)

Basil
30 leaves

 Salt, pepper

**Preparation time:
20 min.
Cooking time: 30 min.**

• Stem and seeded the **red bell peppers**, cut them into pieces, and add them to a saucepan filled with 1¼ cups (300 mL) of water. Turn the heat to medium. Peel the **garlic** and add it to the pan. Simmer for 25 minutes. Blend with a hand blender. Grate the **Parmesan**.

• Boil the **penne** for 11 minutes, just to *al dente*, in lightly salted water. Drain and add to the saucepan with the **red bell peppers** and **garlic**. Sprinkle with grated **Parmesan** and stir in the **basil**. Season with salt and pepper. Heat through for 5 minutes and serve.

SPAGHETTI WITH CLAMS

Clams
1½ quarts (1.5 liters)

Extra-virgin olive oil
¼ cup (60 mL)

Garlic
4 cloves

Flat-leaf parsley
8 sprigs

Spaghetti
10 ounces (300 g)

 Salt, pepper

👤👤👤👤

🕐

**Preparation time:
15 min.
Cooking time: 25 min.**

• Peel and chop the **garlic** and chop all but a few leaves of the **parsley**.
• Heat the clams in a large, dry skillet until they open. Add the **olive oil** and **garlic**.
• Boil the **spaghetti** for 12 minutes, just to *al dente*, in lightly salted water. Drain and transfer to the skillet with the **clams**. Cook over medium-high heat for 5 minutes more, while stirring. Add the chopped **parsley**. Season with salt and pepper, garnish with the parsley leaves, and enjoy.

SPAGHETTI WITH ASPARAGUS AND ORANGE

Green asparagus
x 10

Orange
x 1

Extra-virgin olive oil
¼ cup (60 mL)

Spaghetti
10 ounces (300 g)

Parmesan cheese wedge
3½ ounces (100 g)

 Salt, pepper

**Preparation time:
10 min.
Cooking time: 20 min.**

- Wash the **asparagus**, remove the tough woody ends, and cut in two. Peel the **orange** and cut into pieces.
- In a skillet over medium heat, sauté the **asparagus** with the **olive oil** for 10 minutes.
- Boil the **spaghetti** for 12 minutes, just to *al dente*, in lightly salted water. Grate the **Parmesan**. Drain and add to the skillet. Stir in the **orange** and Parmesan. Heat for an additional 5 minutes, stirring. Season with salt and pepper.

SPAGHETTI BOLOGNAISE WITH CHERRY TOMATOES

Spaghetti
10 ounces (300 g)

Extra-virgin olive oil
2 tablespoons (30 mL)

White onions
x 2

Ground beef
14 ounces (400 g)

Cherry tomatoes
9 ounces (255 g)

Basil
20 leaves

 Salt, pepper

**Preparation time:
10 min.
Cooking time: 50 min.**

- Peel and thinly slice the **onions**. Quarter the **cherry tomatoes**.
- Boil the **spaghetti** for 12 minutes, just to *al dente*, in lightly salted water. Drain and set aside.
- In a large saucepan over medium-high heat, heat the **olive oil**. Add the **onions** and cook, browning, for about 5 minutes.
- Add the **cherry tomatoes** to the saucepan along with 2 cups (480 mL) of water. Simmer on low heat for 30 minutes. Add the **ground beef**, **spaghetti**, and **basil**. Cook for 5 minutes more. Sprinkle with Parmesan, if desired, and enjoy.

SPAGHETTI CARBONARA WITH CRAB

Cilantro
1 bunch

Spaghetti
10 ounces (300 g)

Eggs
x 2

Heavy (whipping) cream
1 cup (240 mL)

Curry powder
1 tablespoon (5 g)

Crab meat
2 cans (6 ounces, 170 g total)

 Salt, pepper

**Preparation time:
15 min.
Cooking time: 14 min.**

- Wash and chop the **cilantro**.
- Boil the **spaghetti** for 12 minutes, just to *al dente*, in lightly salted water. Separate the eggs and reserve the whites for another use. In a skillet, whisk together the **egg** yolks, **cream**, **curry powder**, and **crab**.
- Drain the **spaghetti** and add it to a skillet with the **crab** mixture. Mix well for 2 minutes over low heat to blend the ingredients. Stir in the **cilantro**. Season with salt and pepper and serve. Garnish with an additional egg yolk if desired.

SMOKED SALMON AND SPINACH LASAGNA

Smoked salmon
7 ounces (200 g)

Cream
1¼ cups (300 mL)

Defrosted frozen spinach
1⅓ pounds (600 g)

No-boil lasagna noodles
x 10

Extra-virgin olive oil
2 tablespoons (30 mL)

 Pepper

👤👤👤👤

**Preparation time:
20 min.
Cooking time: 30 min.**

• Preheat the oven to 350°F/180°C. Cut the **salmon** into pieces and toss them together with the **spinach** and **cream** in a bowl. Season with pepper.

• Arrange alternating layers of the **lasagna noodles** and spinach mixture in a baking dish. Bake for 30 minutes, drizzle with the **olive oil**, and enjoy.

TOMATO RISOTTO

Arborio rice
2 cups (400 g)

Chicken stock
2 cups (480 mL)

Dry white wine
1 glass (5 fluid ounces or 150 mL)

Extra-virgin olive oil
6 tablespoons (90 mL)

Cherry tomatoes
9 ounces (255 g)

Parmesan cheese wedge
3½ ounces (100 g)

 **Salt, pepper**

Preparation time: 5 min.
Cooking time: 25 min.

- Wash and chop the **tomatoes**.
- In a large saucepan over low heat, place the **rice**, **chicken broth**, **white wine**, 3 tablespoons (45 mL) of **olive oil**, and the **tomatoes**. Cook, stirring with a spatula, until the **broth** is absorbed, about 20 to 25 minutes. The **rice** should still be firm.
- Grate the **Parmesan** and stir it in, along with the remaining 3 tablespoons (45 mL) of **olive oil**. Stir well to blend all the ingredients.

SAFFRON RISOTTO

Arborio rice
2 cups (400 g)

Chicken stock
2 cups (480 mL)

Dry white wine
1 glass (5 fluid ounces or 150 mL)

Extra-virgin olive oil
6 tablespoons (90 mL)

Saffron
15 threads

Parmesan cheese wedge
3½ ounces (100 g)

 **Salt, pepper**

Preparation time: 5 min.
Cooking time: 25 min.

- In a large saucepan, place the **rice**, **stock**, **white wine**, 3 tablespoons of **olive oil**, and the **saffron threads**. Cook on low heat, stirring with a spatula, until the **broth** is absorbed, about 20 to 25 minutes. The **rice** should still be firm.
- Grate the **Parmesan** and stir it in along with the remaining 3 tablespoons (45 mL) of **olive oil**. Stir to blend the ingredients well.

FRIED RICE WITH SHRIMP AND PORK

Shrimp
x 8

Pork loin chops
x 2 (12 ounces or 350 g each)

Fresh ginger
3 ounces (85 g)

Soy sauce
½ cup (120 mL)

Curry powder
2 tablespoons (10 g)

Cooked rice
2 cups (400 g)

Salt, pepper + pan with oil

👥👥👥👥

🕐

Preparation time: 20 min.
Cooking time: 25 min.

- Shell the **shrimp**. Peel and grate the **ginger**.
- Cut the **pork** into pieces and sauté in a wok over high heat with the oil for about 10 minutes.
- Add the **shrimp**, **ginger**, **rice**, **curry powder**, and **soy sauce**. Continue to cook, stirring occasionally, until the **rice** is browned, about 15 minutes. Season with salt and pepper and enjoy.

PIZZA WITH BUTTON MUSHROOMS

Pizza dough
2 balls (6 ounces/170 g each;
thawed if frozen)

Sour cream
½ cup (115 g)

Baby spinach
7 ounces (200 g)

Button mushrooms
x 16 (large)

**Lemon peel from
preserved lemons**
x 4

Extra-virgin olive oil
½ cup (120 mL)

 Salt, pepper

**Preparation time:
15 min.
Cooking time: 25 min.**

• Preheat the oven to 400°F/210°C. Roll out the **dough** balls on a baking sheet into 8- to 12-inch (20 to 30 cm) rounds. Clean and thinly slice the **mushrooms**. Peel the **lemons** and dice the peel.

• Spread half of the **cream** evenly over each crust. Sprinkle each with half of the **spinach**, half of the **mushrooms**, and diced **lemon** peel. Bake for 25 minutes. Remove; add the remaining **spinach** and **mushrooms**. Drizzle with **olive oil**. Season with salt and pepper, and enjoy.

SPICY PIZZA WITH PEPPERS

Pizza dough
2 balls (6 ounces/170 g each; thawed if frozen)

Red bell peppers
x 4

Chorizo
16 large slices

Mint
4 sprigs

Extra-virgin olive oil
½ cup (120 mL)

  Salt, pepper

⏱

**Preparation time:
15 min.
Cooking time: 25 min.**

• Preheat the oven to 400°F/210°C. Wash the **mint** and remove the leaves. Roll out the **dough** balls on a baking sheet into 8- to 12-inch (20 to 30 cm) rounds. Thinly slice the **red bell peppers**. Cover each crust with half of the **peppers** and half of **chorizo**.

• Bake for 25 minutes. Remove; add the **mint**, drizzle with **olive oil**, season with salt and pepper, and enjoy.

TOMATO AND CHERRY PIZZA

Pizza dough
2 balls (6 ounces/170 g each;
thawed if frozen)

Tapenade
2 tablespoons (30 g)

Cherry tomatoes
x 24

Sour cherries
x 40 (frozen)

Grated mozzarella
3½ ounces (100 g)

Extra-virgin olive oil
2 tablespoons (30 mL)

 Salt, pepper

👤👤👤👤

🕐

**Preparation time:
15 min.
Cooking time: 25 min.**

• Preheat the oven to 425°F/220°C. Cut the **cherry tomatoes** in half. Roll out the **dough** balls on a baking sheet into 8- to 12-inch (20 to 30 cm) rounds.

• Brush each crust with 1 tablespoon (15 g) of **tapenade**. Cover each with **cherry tomatoes** and **sour cherries**. Sprinkle with grated **mozzarella cheese**.

• Bake for 25 minutes. Remove; season with salt and pepper, and drizzle with **olive oil**.

GOAT CHEESE WRAPS WITH TOMATOES AND THYME

Pizza dough
2 balls (6 ounces/170 g each; thawed if frozen)

Goat cheese
x 4 (9 ounces/250 g total)

Tomatoes
x 2 medium

Extra-virgin olive oil
½ cup (120 mL)

Thyme
4 sprigs

 Salt, pepper

Preparation time: 15 min.
Cooking time: 25 min.
Resting time: 5 min.

• Preheat the oven to 425°F/220°C. Slice the **tomatoes**. Cut each **dough** ball in half and roll them out on a baking sheet into 6-inch (15 cm) rounds. In the center of each crust place 1 **goat cheese** and equal amounts of **tomato** slices.

• Season with salt and pepper. Drizzle each with 2 tablespoons (30 mL) of **olive oil**. Sprinkle with **thyme**. Fold the crust to form a wrap, pressing your fingers along the edges to seal. Bake for 25 minutes. Remove, let stand for 5 minutes, and serve with salad, if desired.

PIZZA WITH PROSCIUTTO, DANDELION, AND PEAR

Pizza dough
2 balls (6 ounces/170 g each; thawed if frozen)

Sour cream
¼ cup (60 mL)

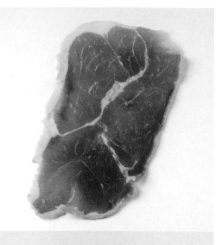

Prosciutto
8 thin slices

Dandelion leaves
7 ounces (200 g)

Pears
x 2

Extra-virgin olive oil
2 tablespoons (30 mL)

  **Salt, pepper**

👤👤👤👤

🕐

Preparation time: 5 min.
Cooking time: 25 min.

• Preheat the oven to 425°F/220°C. Chop the **prosciutto** and thinly slice the **pears**. Roll out the **dough** balls on a baking sheet into 8- to 12-inch (20 to 30 cm) rounds. Layer each with **sour cream** and **prosciutto**.
• Bake for 25 minutes. Remove; add the **dandelion** leaves and **pears**; drizzle with **olive oil**. Season with salt and pepper and enjoy.

ZUCCHINI AND PROSCIUTTO PIZZA WITH PESTO

Pizza dough
2 balls (6 ounces/170 g each;
thawed if frozen)

Pesto
2 tablespoons (30 g)

Zucchini
x 2

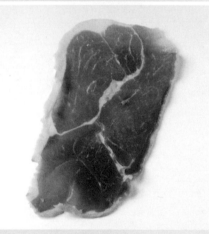

Prosciutto
8 slices

Extra-virgin olive oil
¼ cup (60 mL)

 Salt, pepper

**Preparation time:
15 min.
Cooking time: 25 min.**

• Preheat the oven to 425°F/220°C. Thinly slice the **zucchini** lengthwise. Roll out the **dough** balls on a baking sheet into 8- to 12-inch (20 to 30 cm) rounds. Brush them with **pesto**. Cover with **zucchini** and **prosciutto**. Drizzle with **olive oil**. Season with salt and pepper.

• Bake for 25 minutes. Remove and enjoy.

PROVENÇAL ONION TART

Mild onions
x 6

Extra-virgin olive oil
½ cup (120 mL)

Puff pastry
x 1 sheet

Dried thyme
1 tablespoon (5 g)

Black olives
x 16 (pitted, marinated
à la grecque)

**Preparation time:
20 min.
Cooking time:
1 hr. 5 min.**

• Preheat the oven to 350°F/180°C. Peel and thinly slice the **onions**. Heat the **olive oil** in a skillet over medium heat. Stew the onions for 25 minutes, then remove from the heat and add the **thyme**.

• Unroll the **puff pastry** on a baking sheet lined with parchment paper. Spread the onions evenly over the pastry, top with the **olives**, and bake for 30 minutes. Enjoy hot or cold.

POTATO TURNOVER

Potatoes
about 1 pound (500 g)

Sour cream
¾ cup (200 mL)

Cooked ham
4 slices

Grated nutmeg
½ teaspoon

Rosemary
1 sprig

Puff pastry
x 1 sheet

**Preparation time:
20 min.
Cooking time: 40 min.**

• Preheat the oven to 350°F/180°C. Peel and thinly slice the **potatoes**. Strip the leaves from the **rosemary sprig** and chop them. Dice the **ham**. Mix the potatoes, rosemary, ham, **cream**, and **nutmeg** in a bowl. Unroll the **puff pastry** on a baking sheet lined with parchment paper. Spread the potato mixture over one half of the pastry and fold the other half over the top to cover. Press the edges of the pastry with the tines of a fork to seal. Bake for 40 minutes. Enjoy hot or cold.

LEEK AND PARMESAN TART

Leeks
x 5 (small)

Puff pastry
x 1 sheet

Coarsely grated Parmesan cheese
1¼ cups (100 g)

Sour cream
2 tablespoons (15 mL)

Extra-virgin olive oil
2 tablespoons (30 mL)

 Salt, pepper

👤👤👤👤

Preparation time:
15 min.
Cooking time: 40 min.

- Preheat the oven to 350°F/180°C. Trim the root ends of the **leeks**, slit lengthwise, and wash thoroughly.
- Line a long tart pan with **puff pastry**. Cover with the leeks and then the **Parmesan**, **cream**, and **olive oil**. Season with salt and pepper.
- Bake for 40 minutes. Serve hot with a green salad, if desired.

126

CHERRY TOMATO AND MUSTARD TARTLETS

Puff pastry
x 1 sheet

Dijon mustard
¼ cup (45 g)

Cherry tomatoes
x 32

Extra-virgin olive oil
¼ cup (60 mL)

Thyme
4 sprigs

 Salt, pepper

**Preparation time:
10 min.
Cooking time: 35 min.**

• Preheat the oven to 350°F/180°C. Cut the **cherry tomatoes** in half. With a pizza cutter, cut out 4 circles of **pastry** about 5 inches (12 cm) wide and place them into small tart molds. Garnish each with 1 tablespoon (11 g) of **mustard**, 16 **cherry tomato** halves, and 1 tablespoon (15 mL) of **olive oil**.

• Sprinkle with **thyme**; season with salt and pepper. Bake for 35 minutes. Serve hot or cold.

SMOKED SALMON AND RICOTTA PIZZA

Pizza dough
2 balls (6 ounces/170 g each; thawed if frozen)

Ricotta
1 cup (250 g)

Smoked salmon
4 slices

Green apples
x 2

Chives
1 bunch

Lemon
x 1

 Salt, pepper

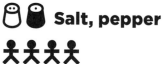

**Preparation time:
15 min.
Cooking time: 25 min.**

• Preheat the oven to 425°F/220°C. Chop the **smoked salmon**. Julienne the **apples**. Finely chop the **chives**. Roll the **dough** balls on a baking sheet into 8- to 12-inch (20 to 30 cm) rounds. Cover each with **ricotta** and bake for 25 minutes.
• Remove; cover each with **smoked salmon**, **apples**, and **chives**. Squeeze **lemon** juice over. Season with salt and pepper and enjoy.

BACON AND SAGE PIZZA

Pizza dough
2 balls (6 ounces/170 g each; thawed if frozen)

Sour cream
4 tablespoons (60 mL)

Bacon
7 thin slices

Sage
2 sprigs

Extra-virgin olive oil
¼ cup (60 mL)

 Salt, pepper

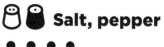

Preparation time: 15 min.
Cooking time: 25 min.

• Preheat the oven to 425°F/220°C. Wash the **sage** and remove the leaves. Roll out the **dough** balls on a baking sheet into 8- to 12-inch (20 to 30 cm) rounds. Cover with the **sour cream**, **bacon** slices, and **sage**.

• Bake for 25 minutes. Remove; drizzle with **olive oil**. Season with salt and pepper and enjoy.

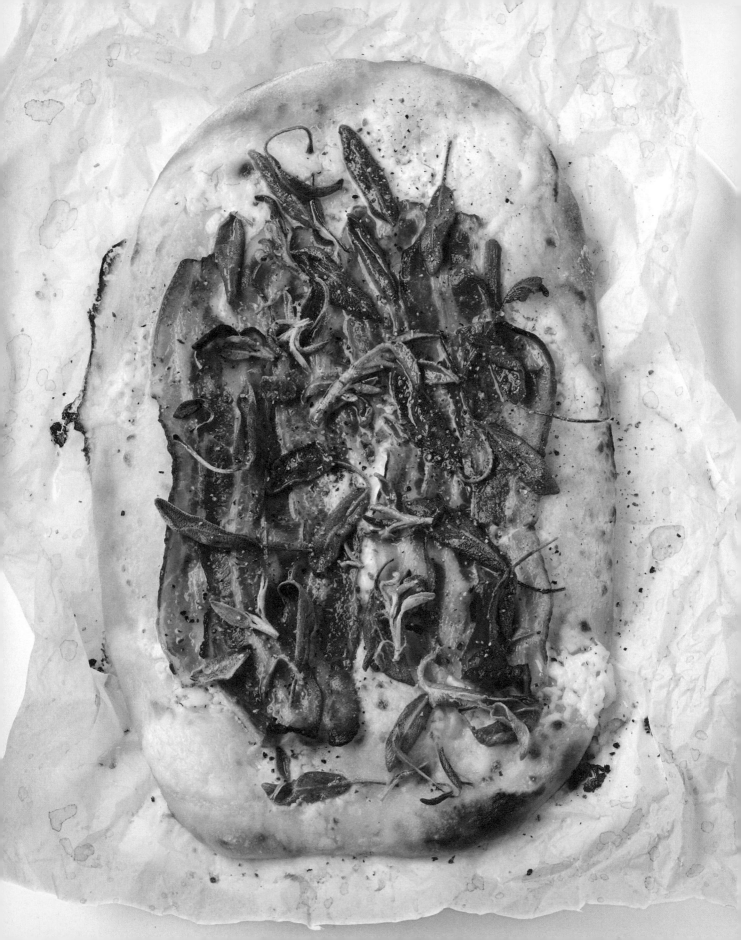

SPINACH AND SALMON TARTLETS

Eggs
x 3

Cream
1¼ cups (300 mL)

Grated Parmesan cheese
1 cup (100 g)

Spinach
3 ounces (90 g)

Puff pastry
x 1 sheet

Salmon steaks
7 ounces (200 g)

**Preparation time:
15 min.
Cooking time: 35 min.**

• Preheat the oven to 350°F/180°C. Beat the **eggs** with the **cream** and **cheese**. Bring a saucepan of water to a boil. Blanch the **spinach** in the boiling water for 1 minute, then drain and squeeze out excess water. Cut the **salmon** into bite-size pieces.

• Unroll the **pastry**. Using a 4-inch tart pan as a guide, cut out four circles of pastry, making sure to cut them slightly larger than the mold. Place the circles of pastry in the molds. Fill with the cream, spinach, and salmon. Bake for 35 minutes. Enjoy hot or cold.

BAKED POLENTA WITH OLIVES

Polenta
1⅓ cups (240 g)

Grated Parmesan cheese
1½ cups (150 g)

Olives
x 30 (pitted)

Oregano
1 tablespoon

Sun-dried tomatoes
x 25

Extra-virgin olive oil
5 tablespoons (75 mL)

**Preparation time:
15 min., plus 1 hr.
chilling time
Cooking time: 25 min.**

• Bring 4 cups (1 L) salted water to a boil. Chop the **olives** and the **sun-dried tomatoes**. Gradually pour the **polenta** into the boiling water. Whisk until it thickens. Add 1 cup (100 g) of the **cheese**, the olives, tomatoes, and **oregano**. Line a baking pan with a sheet of moistened parchment paper and pour in the polenta. Set aside in a cool place to firm up. Preheat the oven to 350°F/180°C. Slice the set polenta and transfer to a gratin dish. Drizzle with the **olive oil**, sprinkle with the remaining cheese, and bake for 10 minutes. Enjoy hot or cold.

COLD MINT RATATOUILLE

White onion
x 1

Assorted bell peppers
x 2

Zucchini
x 2

Eggplant
x 1 (small)

Extra-virgin olive oil
6 tablespoons (90 mL)

Mint
20 leaves

Salt, pepper

**Preparation time:
25 min.
Cooking time: 45 min.**

• Peel and chop the **onion**. Seed and dice the **peppers**. Dice the **zucchini**, and **eggplant**. Finely chop the **mint**.
• In a skillet over medium heat, heat the **olive oil**. Briefly sauté the **vegetables**, but do not brown them. Season with salt and pepper. Cover, reduce the heat to low, and cook for 30 minutes without letting the mixture brown. Uncover and cook for a further 15 minutes. Cool, add the **mint**, and enjoy.

VEGETABLE TIAN

Potatoes
x 2 (large)

Eggplant
x 1

Zucchini
x 2

Tomatoes
x 3

Fresh thyme
2 tablespoon (10 g)

Extra-virgin olive oil
6 tablespoons (90 mL)

Salt, pepper

**Preparation time:
15 min.
Cooking time: 45 min.**

• Preheat the oven to 350°F/180°C. Thinly slice all the vegetables. Arrange them in layers a baking dish. Season with salt, pepper, and **thyme**. Drizzle the **olive oil** over.
• Bake for 45 minutes and serve in the dish.

EGGPLANT GRATIN

Eggplant
x 2

Mozzarella
2 balls (9 ounces/250 g total)

Crushed tomatoes
1 can (10 ounces or 300 g)

Shredded Parmesan cheese
1¼ cups (100 g)

Extra-virgin olive oil
2 tablespoons (30 mL)

 **Salt, pepper**

👤👤👤👤

🕐

**Preparation time:
25 min.
Cooking time: 1 hr.**

• Preheat the oven to 350°F/180°C. Slice the **eggplant** and the **mozzarella**.
• Alternate layers of **tomato**, **mozzarella**, and **eggplant** in a baking dish. Season with salt and pepper. Sprinkle with **Parmesan** and drizzle with **olive oil**.
• Bake for 1 hour and serve with a salad, if desired.

SWISS CHARD GRATIN WITH CHEESE

Swiss chard
2 pounds (1 kg)

Heavy (whipping) cream
2½ cups (600 mL)

Grated cheese
7 ounces (200 g)

  Salt, pepper

**Preparation time:
15 min.
Cooking time: 30 min.**

• Preheat the oven to 350°F/180°C. Wash the **Swiss chard** and cut it into pieces. Plunge them in lightly salted boiling water for 5 minutes, drain, cool, and combine with the **cream**, **cheese**, salt, and pepper.

• Transfer the mixture to a baking dish and bake for 30 minutes. When nicely browned, remove and serve in the dish with a salad, if desired.

ZUCCHINI BEIGNETS WITH SALAD

Arugula
2 handfuls (80 g)

Zucchini
x 2

Eggs
x 2, separated

Flour
¾ cup (100 g)

Beer
32 fluid ounces (1 L)

Mint
10 leaves

 **Salt, pepper
+ 1 skillet with ⅓ cup
(80 mL) frying oil**

**Preparation time:
15 min.
Cooking time: 5 min.**

• Wash the **arugula**. Slice the **zucchini**. Wash and chop the **mint**. Beat the **egg whites** until stiff.

• Heat the oil over high heat to 350°F/180°C. Mix together the **flour**, **beer**, and **egg yolks**. Fold in the **egg whites**. Dip the **zucchini** into the beer batter and fry until golden, about 5 minutes. Enjoy the beignets hot with the **arugula** and **mint**.

ZUCCHINI GRATIN

Zucchini
1½ pounds (680 g)

Grated cheese
7 ounces (200 g)

 Salt, pepper

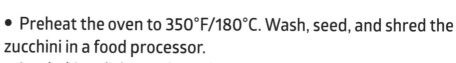

Preparation time: 5 min.
Cooking time: 30 min.

• Preheat the oven to 350°F/180°C. Wash, seed, and shred the zucchini in a food processor.
• In a baking dish, combine the **zucchini** with the **grated cheese**. Season with salt and pepper. Bake for 30 minutes or until brown.

CARAMELIZED TURNIPS WITH HONEY

Baby turnips
2 bunches

Honey
¾ cup (255 g)

 **Salt, pepper**

👥👥👥👥

🕐

**Preparation time:
15 min.
Cooking time: 40 min.**

• Clean and peel the **turnips**. Boil them for 30 minutes in salted water. (They should be tender).

• In a large pan over medium-high heat, warm the **honey**. Add the **turnips**. Caramelize over high heat, stirring, 6 to 8 minutes. Season with salt and pepper and serve as a side dish.

ROASTED POTATO WEDGES WITH SALT AND ROSEMARY

Potatoes
2 pounds (1 kg), with firm skins

Extra-virgin olive oil
6 tablespoons (90 mL)

Rosemary
2 sprigs

Sea salt
1½ tablespoons (30 g)

 Pepper

👤👤👤👤

🕐

Preparation time: 10 min.
Cooking time: 30 min.

• Preheat the oven to 350°F/180°C. Wash the **potatoes**, cut them into wedges, and arrange on a baking sheet. Drizzle with **olive oil**. Bake for 30 minutes, turning them midway to brown both sides.

• Chop the **rosemary** and mix it with the **sea salt**. Toss the hot wedges in the seasoned salt. Serve with ketchup, if desired.

SWEET POTATO FRIES

Avocados
x 2

Lemons
x 2

Sweet potatoes
2 pounds (1 kg)

Sea salt
1½ tablespoons (30 g)

Curry powder
4 teaspoons (15 g)

+ skillet with enough frying oil to generously cover the bottom

**Preparation time: 15 min.
Cooking time: 25 min.**

• Peel and pit the **avocados**. Juice the **lemons**, straining out any seeds. Scoop out the **avocado** flesh and mash it well with the **lemon** juice. Season with salt and pepper and refrigerate.

• Peel the **sweet potatoes** and slice them evenly into sticks. Heat the skillet of oil over high heat. Fry the **sweet potatoes** for 15 to 20 minutes, or until browned. Drain on paper towels. Toss with the **salt** and **curry powder**. Enjoy with the **avocado** dip.

DAUPHINOISE GRATIN

Garlic
2 cloves

Potatoes
2 pounds (1 kg)

Heavy cream
1¾ cups (420 mL)

Grated nutmeg
½ teaspoon

 Salt, pepper

**Preparation time:
15 min.
Cooking time: 1 hr.**

- Preheat the oven to 325°F/170°C. Peel the **garlic** and **potatoes** and thinly slice both.
- Layer the **potatoes** in a gratin dish with the **garlic** and **cream**. Season with salt, pepper, and **nutmeg** between the layers, finishing with the **cream**.
- Bake for 1 hour. Enjoy piping hot.

TARTIFLETTE WITH GOUDA CHEESE AND CUMIN SEEDS

White onion
x 1

Potatoes
x 4 (large)

Lardons of bacon
7 ounces (200 g)

**Gouda cheese
with cumin seeds**
14 ounces (400 g)

Cumin seeds
1 teaspoon

Salt, pepper

**Preparation time:
10 min.
Cooking time: 30 min.**

• Preheat the oven to 325°F/170°C. Peel and slice the **onion** into slivers. Peel and cut the **potatoes** into thin strips.
• Arrange the **potatoes**, diced **bacon**, and **onion** in a baking dish. Cover with **Gouda** and sprinkle with the **cumin seeds**. Bake for 30 minutes and serve.

BELL PEPPERS STUFFED WITH RICOTTA AND OLIVES

Ricotta
2 pots (9 ounces or 255 g each)

Powdered thyme
1 teaspoon

Tapenade
2 tablespoons (30 g)

Green bell peppers
x 2 (large)

Tomato purée
16 fluid ounces (480 mL)

  Salt, pepper

👤👤👤👤

🕐

**Preparation time:
10 min.
Cooking time: 40 min.**

• Preheat the oven to 350°F/180°C. Combine the **ricotta**, **thyme**, and **tapenade**.

• Cut the **peppers** in half, remove the seeds, and fill them with the ricotta-tapenade mixture.

• In a baking dish, whisk the **tomato purée** with 1 cup (240 mL) of water. Place the **peppers** on top, and season with salt and pepper. Bake for 40 minutes. Enjoy hot or cold.

BAKED PEPPERS WITH PARSLEY SAUCE

Assorted bell peppers
x 8

Flat-leaf parsley
8 sprigs

Garlic
6 cloves

Extra-virgin olive oil
6 tablespoons (90 mL)

 **Salt, pepper**

👤👤👤👤

🕐

**Preparation time:
20 min.
Cooking time: 30 min.**

- Preheat the oven to 350°F/180°C. Peel and crush the **garlic**. Wash and chop the **parsley**.
- Bake the **bell peppers** for 30 minutes. Take them out of the oven, remove their seeds, and pour any juices into a mixing bowl. Add the **bell peppers** to the bowl, along with the **olive oil**, **garlic**, and **parsley**. Season with salt and pepper. Mix and enjoy!

MOZZARELLA AND FIG KEBABS

Arugula
2 handfuls

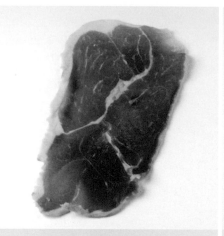

Prosciutto
4 slices

Mozzarella
1 ball (4½ ounces or 130 g)

Fresh figs
x 4

Extra-virgin olive oil
¼ cup (60 mL)

 Salt, pepper

👤👤👤👤

🕐

**Preparation time:
10 min.
Cooking time: 5 min.**

• Preheat the oven to 350°F/180°C. Wash the **arugula**. Quarter the **prosciutto**. Slice the **mozzarella** into eight pieces and each **fig** into three pieces.
• Alternate the ingredients on skewers. Place the skewers in a baking dish and bake for 5 minutes. Arrange them on platter with the **arugula**, drizzle with **olive oil**, and season with salt and pepper.

TOMATO-EGG BAKE

Tomatoes
x 4 (large)

Extra-virgin olive oil
¼ cup (60 mL)

Eggs
x 8

Balsamic vinegar
2 tablespoons (30 mL)

 Salt, pepper

👤👤👤👤

🕐
Preparation time: 5 min.
Cooking time: 15 min.

• Preheat the oven to 325°F/170°C. Cut the **tomatoes** in half; core and seed them. Place in a baking dish, drizzle with **olive oil**, and bake for 5 minutes.

• Break 1 **egg** into each tomato half. Season with salt and pepper. Bake for 10 minutes more. Add a dash of **balsamic vinegar** and serve.

LEEK GRATIN WITH CHEESE

Leeks
14 ounces (400 g)

Mozzarella and cheddar
about 9 ounces (255 g) total

 Salt, pepper

👤👤👤👤

🕐

**Preparation time:
10 min.
Cooking time: 30 min.**

• Preheat the oven to 350°F/180°C. Cut the root ends off the **leeks**, split lengthwise, wash thoroughly in water, dry, and place in a baking dish.

• Cut the **cheese** into slices and layer on top of the **leeks**. Bake for 30 minutes. When the leeks are browned, remove the dish and enjoy with a salad, if desired.

PEAR GRATIN WITH PARMESAN

Pears
x 4

Parmesan cheese wedge
3½ ounces (100 g)

 **Salt, pepper**

👤👤👤👤

🕐

Preparation time: 5 min.
Cooking time: 30 min.

- Preheat the oven to 350°F/180°C. Peel and quarter the **pears**. Roughly chop the **Parmesan** into pieces.
- Place the **pears** in a baking dish; cover with **Parmesan**. Season lightly with salt and pepper. Bake for 30 minutes until brown.
- Enjoy as an appetizer or serve with a salad, poultry, or roast veal, if desired.

LAMB STEW WITH VEGETABLES

Lamb stew meat
2¾ pounds (1.25 kg), shoulder or leg of lamb

Extra-virgin olive oil
¼ cup (60 mL)

Thyme
2 sprigs

Crushed tomatoes
1 can (28 ounces or 800 g)

Green peas
1 cup (225 g), fresh or frozen

Snow peas
7 ounces (200 g)

 **Salt, pepper**

👤👤👤👤

🕐

Preparation time: 5 min.
Cooking time:
1 hr., 25 min.

• In a large pan over high heat, sear the **lamb** with the olive **oil**, about 10 minutes.
• Reduce the heat to medium and add the **thyme**, **tomatoes**, salt, and pepper. Reduce the heat to low, cover, and simmer for 1 hour. Add the **green peas** and **snow peas**. Cover and cook for 20 minutes more.

LAMB AND POTATO BAKE

Potatoes
x 2 (large)

White onions
x 2

Tomatoes
x 3

Lamb shoulder
1⅓ pounds or 600 g

Dried Thyme
2 teaspoons

White wine
1 glass (5 fluid ounces or 150 mL)

Salt, pepper

**Preparation time:
10 min.
Cooking time: 2 hr.**

• Preheat the oven to 325°F/170°C. Peel and cut the **potatoes** and **onions** into thin slices. Cut the **tomatoes** into slices and the **lamb** into large pieces.

• Combine all the ingredients in a large Dutch oven. Season with salt and pepper. Add the **white wine** and 1¼ cups (300 mL) of water. Bake for 2 hours.

LAMB KEBABS WITH MANGO

Mint
30 leaves (small)

Mangoes
x 2

Lamb shoulder
1¾ pounds (800 g)

Extra-virgin olive oil
¼ cup (60 mL)

Balsamic vinegar
¼ cup (60 mL)

Salt, pepper

Preparation time: 10 min.
Cooking time: 20 min.

• Preheat the oven to 350°F/180°C. Wash the **mint**. Peel the **mangoes** and cut them and the **lamb** into small pieces. Alternate placing the **lamb** and **mangoes** on skewers.
• Roast the skewers for 20 minutes under the broiler.
• Arrange them on a dish, drizzle with **olive oil** and **balsamic vinegar**, sprinkle with **mint**, season with salt and pepper, and enjoy.

ROASTED LAMB SHOULDER

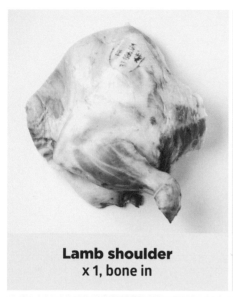

Lamb shoulder
x 1, bone in

Flat-leaf parsley
6 sprigs

Cilantro
1 bunch

Garlic
6 cloves

Green chile
x 1

Extra-virgin olive oil
5 fluid ounces (150 mL)

🧂 🧂 **Salt, pepper**

👤👤👤👤

🕐
**Preparation time:
15 min.
Cooking time: 2 hr.**

• Preheat the oven to 325°F/160°C. Place the **lamb** in a large casserole dish and season with salt and pepper. Bake for 2 hours, basting from time to time.

• Wash the **parsley** and **cilantro**; remove the leaves. Peel the **garlic**. Remove the seeds from the **chile**. Use a blender to blend these ingredients with the **olive oil** to make the sauce. Enjoy the **lamb** with the sauce and an arugula salad on the side, if desired.

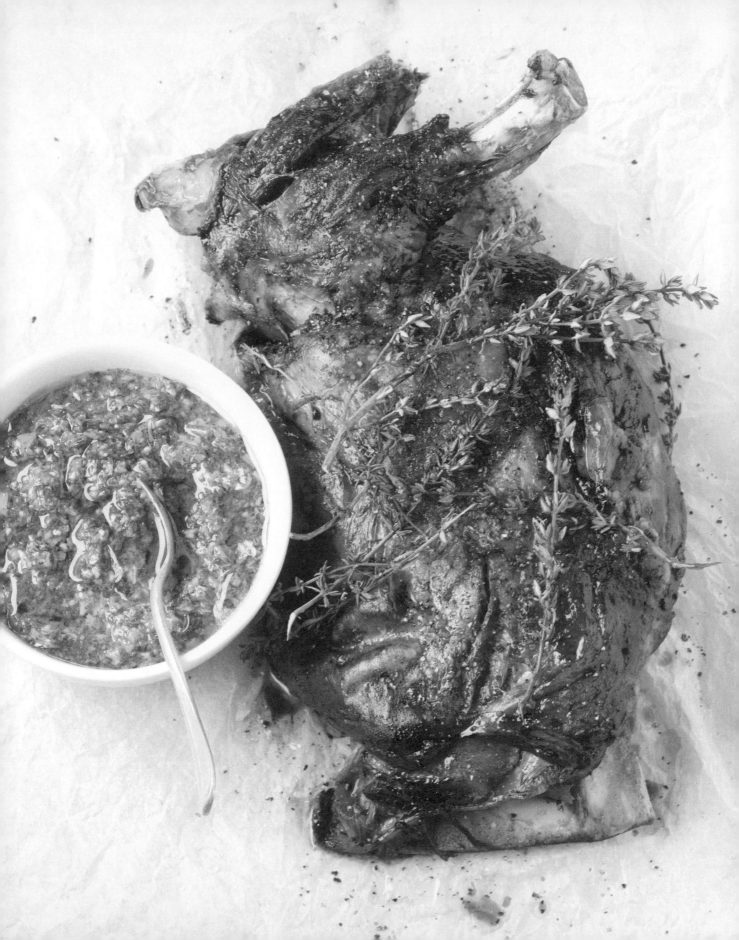

SEVEN-HOUR LAMB

Leg of lamb
x 1

Garlic
10 cloves

Dessert wine
½ bottle (12½ fluid ounces
or 375 mL)

Chicken stock
16 fluid ounces (480 mL)

Rosemary
2 sprigs

Red port
½ bottle (12½ fluid ounces
or 375 mL)

Salt, pepper

**Preparation time:
10 min.
Cooking time: 7 hr.**

- Preheat the oven to 325°F/160°C. Peel and crush the **garlic**.
- Place the **leg of lamb** in a large lidded cast-iron pot. Add the **garlic**, **dessert wine**, **red port**, **stock**, and **rosemary**. Cover and bake for 7 hours, basting occasionally. Add water if the sauce reduces too much. Serve the **lamb** ladled with sauce, accompanied by couscous, if desired.

VEAL RAGOUT WITH ASPARAGUS

Veal stew meat pieces
2¾ pounds (1.25 kg)

Water or broth
16 fluid ounces (480 mL)

Green asparagus
x 4 (large)

Button mushrooms
7 ounces (200 g)

Light cream
1½ cups (360 mL)

Flour
2 tablespoons (31 g)

 Salt, pepper

👤👤👤👤

🕐
**Preparation time:
15 min.**
**Cooking time:
1 hr., 15 min.**

• In a large saucepan over low heat, cook the **veal** for 1 hour in the **broth**. Peel the **asparagus** and cut it into pieces. Thinly slice the **mushrooms**.

• Remove the meat from the **broth**. Combine the **cream** with the **flour** and whisk this into the **broth**. Add the **asparagus** and **mushrooms**. Cook for 10 minutes more, while stirring. Return the meat to the sauce. Season with salt and pepper.

VEAL CUTLETS WITH MOREL MUSHROOMS

Dried morel mushrooms
1¾ ounces (50 g)

Heavy (whipping) cream
1½ cups (360 mL)

Veal cutlets, bone-in
x 2 (1 pound or 455 g each)

Soy sauce
¼ cup (60 mL)

🧂🧂 **Salt, pepper**

👤👤👤👤

🕐

Soaking time: 30 min.
Preparation time:
35 min.
Cooking time: 30 min.

• Soak the **mushrooms** for 30 minutes in 2 cups (480 mL) of water. Drain, reserving the liquid. Strain the water and boil it until reduced by three-fourths, about 10 minutes. Add the **cream**. Continue reducing for 10 minutes more over high heat, whisking.

• In a high-sided skillet over high heat, sear the **veal cutlets** for 5 minutes on each side. Leave the cutlets in the pan and deglaze with the **soy sauce**, scraping up any browned bits. Add the **mushrooms** and **cream**. Cook for 5 minutes more. Season with salt and pepper and serve.

VEAL CUTLETS WITH ASPARAGUS

Green asparagus
x 15

Veal scaloppini
x 4 (about 6 ounces/170 g each)

Pesto
2 tablespoons (30 g)

Extra-virgin olive oil
2 tablespoons (30 mL)

 Salt, pepper

👤👤👤👤

🕐

**Preparation time:
10 min.
Cooking time: 30 min.**

• Preheat the oven to 350°F/180°C. Wash the **asparagus** and remove the tough woody ends. Blanch for 3 minutes in boiling water.

• Brush the **veal cutlets** with **pesto**. Place equal amounts of **asparagus** in the center of each. Season with salt and pepper. Wrap the veal into bundles and tie with kitchen string. Drizzle with **olive oil**. Bake for 25 minutes. Cut in thick slices to serve.

VEAL SCALLOPS WITH CHORIZO

Veal scaloppini
x 4 (about 6 ounces/170 g each)

Chorizo
4 slices

Thyme
8 sprigs

Sage
4 leaves

 Salt, pepper

**Preparation time:
10 min.
Cooking time: 25 min.**

• Preheat the oven to 350°F/180°C. Cut the **veal cutlets** in half, and place a slice of **chorizo** on each cutlet (secure with a wooden skewer).

• Add the **thyme**, **sage**, salt, and pepper. Bake for 25 minutes. Serve accompanied by an arugula salad or fresh pasta, as desired.

OSSO BUCCO WITH TOMATOES AND ORANGES

Oranges
x 4

Extra-virgin olive oil
¼ cup (60 mL)

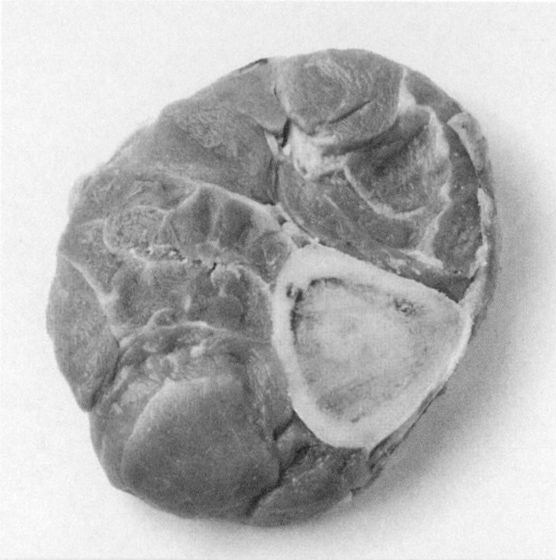

Veal shanks, cross-cut
x 8 (about 6 ounces/170 g each)

Rosemary
2 sprigs

Crushed tomatoes
1 can (28 ounces or 800 g)

Salt, pepper

Preparation time:
15 min.

Cooking time:
1 hr., 30 min.

- Zest the **oranges** and squeeze out their juice. Heat the **olive oil** in a large saucepan. Brown the **shanks** on both sides over high heat, about 10 minutes. Add the orange juice and zest, **rosemary**, and **tomatoes**. Season with salt and pepper.
- Simmer for 1 hour, 30 minutes on low heat. Serve from the pan with fresh pasta, if desired.

ROAST VEAL WITH ASPARAGUS

Green asparagus
x 20

Tarragon
1 bunch

Extra-virgin olive oil
¼ cup (60 mL)

Veal roast
2 pounds (1 kg)

Garlic
4 cloves

 **Salt, pepper**

👤👤👤👤

🕐

**Preparation time:
15 min.
Cooking time: 40 min.**

• Wash the **asparagus** and remove the tough woody ends. Wash the **tarragon**, remove the leaves, and roughly chop. Heat the **olive oil** in a Dutch oven over medium heat. Brown the **veal roast** with the **garlic**, about 5 minutes. Season with salt and pepper. Cover the pot and cook for 25 minutes.
• Add 5 fluid ounces (150 mL) of water and the **asparagus**. Cook for 10 minutes more, and then add the **tarragon**. Mix and serve the roast in slices.

SAUTÉ OF VEAL WITH OLIVES

Extra-virgin olive oil
¼ cup (60 mL)

Veal stew meat pieces
2 pounds (1 kg)

Dry white wine
½ bottle (12½ fluid ounces
or 375 mL)

Bouquet garni
x 1

Tomato purée
16 fluid ounces (480 mL)

Green and black olives
7 ounces (200 g), pitted

Salt, pepper

**Preparation time:
15 min.
Cooking time: 2 hr.**

• In a large saucepan over high heat, heat the **olive oil**,
Brown the **veal**, about 5 minutes. Reduce the heat to medium-
low and add the **white wine**, **bouquet garni**, **tomato
purée**, and pitted **olives**.

• Cover and simmer for 2 hours on low heat, stirring
occasionally. Add a little water if the sauce reduces too much.
Enjoy accompanied by fresh pasta, if desired.

FLANK STEAK WITH CRISPY SHALLOTS

Shallots
x 4 (long)

Milk
1 tablespoon plus 1 teaspoon
(20 mL)

Flour
1 tablespoon (15 g)

Flat-leaf parsley
8 sprigs

Flank steak
x 4 (about 6 ounces or 180g each)

Salt, pepper
+ sauté pan with
2 inches of frying oil

Preparation time:
15 min.
Cooking time: 10 min.

• Wash and chop the **parsley**. Peel and thinly slice the **shallots**. Heat the oil in a skillet over high heat.

• Dip the **shallots** in the **milk** and then in the **flour**. Fry until golden, about 3 minutes.

• In a separate pan, sear the **flank steaks** with 1 tablespoon (30 mL) of oil for 2 minutes on each side for a very rare steak. Arrange on a platter. Top with the **shallots** and **parsley**. Enjoy with a salad, if desired.

BEEF BOURGUIGNON

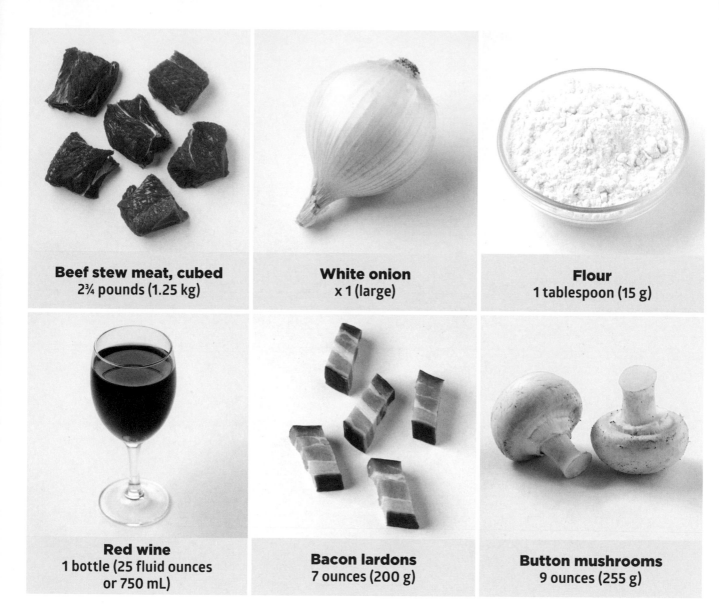

Beef stew meat, cubed
2¾ pounds (1.25 kg)

White onion
x 1 (large)

Flour
1 tablespoon (15 g)

Red wine
1 bottle (25 fluid ounces
or 750 mL)

Bacon lardons
7 ounces (200 g)

Button mushrooms
9 ounces (255 g)

**Salt, pepper
+ pan with oil**

**Preparation time: 10 min.
Cooking time: 2 hr.,
40 min.**

• Peel and thinly slice the **onion**. Wash and chop the **mushrooms**. In a cast-iron pan, heat the oil over high heat.
• Brown the **beef** on all sides, about 5 to 7 minutes. Add the **onion** and **flour**. Cook for 5 minutes more. Pour in the **red wine** and 1¼ cups (300 mL) of water. Cover and simmer for 2 hours over very low heat. Add the **bacon** and **mushrooms**. Cook for 30 minutes more. Season with salt and pepper.

BEEF WITH CARROTS

Carrots
2 pounds (1 kg)

White onions
x 2

Extra-virgin olive oil
3 tablespoons (45 mL)

Flatiron steak
2¾ pounds (1.25 kg)

Thyme
4 sprigs

Bay leaves
3

 Salt, pepper

**Preparation time:
10 min.
Cooking time: 2 hr.**

- Peel and slice the **carrots** into thick pieces. Peel and thinly slice the **onions**.
- In a large saucepan over high heat, heat the **olive oil** to the smoke point. Brown the **steak**, about 5 to 7 minutes. Add the **carrots**, **onions**, **thyme**, and **bay leaves**.
- Season with salt and pepper and add enough water to cover. Simmer for 2 hours on very low heat.

SEASONED BEEF MEATBALLS

Basil
20 leaves

White onion
x 1

Ground beef
1½ pounds (680 g)

Ketchup
¼ cup (60 mL)

Extra-virgin olive oil
¼ cup (60 mL)

Gazpacho
1¼ cups (300 mL)

 **Salt, pepper**

👤👤👤👤

🕐

**Preparation time:
20 min.
Cooking time: 15 min.**

• Preheat the oven to 350°F/180°C. Wash and chop the **basil**. Peel and thinly slice the **onion**.
• In a large bowl, mix all of the ingredients, except the **gazpacho**. Season with salt and pepper. Shape into 12 meatballs. Bake for 15 minutes. Divide the **gazpacho** among 4 soup bowls. Add the hot meatballs and enjoy.

BEEF POT-AU-FEU

Beef cheeks
x 2 (about 2 pounds or 900 g total)

Thyme
4 sprigs

Baby gold turnips
x 6

White beets
x 4 (small)

Sweet potatoes
x 1

 Salt, pepper

👨👨👨👨

🕐

**Preparation time:
10 min.**

**Cooking time: 2 hr.,
50 min.**

• Peel the vegetables. Dice the **sweet potatoes** and set aside. Into a large saucepan, place the whole **turnips**, **whole beets**, **beef**, and **thyme**. Cover everything with water. Cook over very low heat for 2½ hours, regularly skimming the fat off the top.

• Add the **sweet potatoes**. Cook for 20 minutes more. Season with salt and pepper and enjoy.

CHILI CON CARNE

Red onions
x 2

Ground beef
1⅓ pounds (600 g)

Paprika
2 tablespoons (15 g)

Red kidney beans
2 cans (14 ounces or 400 g each)

Tomato purée
16 fluid ounces (480 mL)

Salt, pepper + pan plus oil

Preparation time: 15 min.
Cooking time: 55 min.

• Drain the **kidney beans**. Peel and chop the **onions**. Sauté the **beef** and **onions** in the oil over medium-high heat, about 5 minutes. Add the **paprika**. Cook, browning, for 5 minutes more. Add the **kidney beans** and **tomato purée**. Cook for 45 minutes over low heat, stirring occasionally. Season with salt and pepper. Enjoy topped with avocado slices, if desired.

RIB-EYE STEAK WITH FAUX BÉARNAISE

Mayonnaise
Scant 1 cup (200 g)

Tarragon mustard
1 tablespoon (15 mL)

Red wine vinegar
1 tablespoon (15 mL)

Tarragon
1 bunch

Thick rib-eye steak
x 1 (2 pounds or 1 kg)

 **Salt, pepper
+ pan plus oil**

👤👤👤👤

🕐

**Preparation time:
15 min.
Cooking time: 15 min.
Resting time: 5 min.**

• Preheat the oven to 350°F/180°C. Wash and chop the **tarragon**. Combine it with the **mayonnaise**, **mustard**, and **vinegar** and set aside.
• In an ovenproof skillet over high heat, heat the oil. Brown the **steak** for 1 minute on all sides. Season with salt and pepper. Bake for 10 minutes, turning once.
• Remove, cover loosely with aluminum foil, and let stand for 5 minutes. Enjoy with the sauce.

PROVENÇAL STEW

Basil
1 sprig

Sun-dried tomatoes
x 10

Extra-virgin olive oil
¼ cup (60 mL)

Beef stew meat
2¾ pounds (1.25 kg)

Garlic
4 cloves

Red wine
1 bottle (25 fluid ounces
or 750 mL)

Salt, pepper

**Preparation time:
25 min.
Cooking time: 2 hr.**

• Wash the **basil** and remove the leaves. Chop the **sun-dried tomatoes**. Crush the garlic, leaving the peel on.
• In a large saucepan over medium-high heat, heat the **oil**. Brown the **beef** on all sides, about 5 to 7 minutes. Add the **garlic** with its skin and the **red wine**. Cover and simmer for 2 hours over very low heat. Season with salt and pepper. Mix in the **basil** and **sun-dried tomatoes**. Enjoy with fresh pasta, if desired.

ORANGE BEEF MEATBALLS

Oranges
x 2

Ground beef
1⅓ pounds (600 g)

Parmesan cheese
3½ ounces (100 g)

Dried oregano
2 tablespoons (6 g)

Extra-virgin olive oil
6 tablespoons (90 mL)

 Salt, pepper

👤👤👤👤

🕐
**Preparation time:
10 min.
Cooking time: 15 min.**

• Preheat the oven to 375°F/200°C. Zest and juice the **oranges**, straining out any seeds. Pulse the **meat**, **cheese**, orange zest, and **oregano** in a food processor until just combined. Season with salt and pepper, and shape the meat mixture into 1-inch balls.

• Arrange them on a baking sheet and sprinkle with half the **olive oil**. Bake for 15 minutes. Shortly before serving, drizzle the balls with the remaining oil and the orange juice.

PESTO BURGER

Ground beef
1⅓ pounds (600 g)

Pesto
2 tablespoons (30 mL)

Bacon
8 slices

Hamburger bun
x 4

Tomatoes
x 2 medium

Basil
20 leaves

**extra-virgin olive oil
+ 1 pan with oil**

👤👤👤👤

⏱

**Preparation time:
10 min.
Cooking time: 10 min.**

• Preheat the oven to 350°F/180°C. Mix the **ground beef** with the **pesto** and shape into four patties. Heat 1 tablespoon oil in a skillet over high heat. Cook the **bacon**, drain the fat from the pan, and then cook the burgers for 5 minutes. Toast the **hamburger buns**. Cut each **tomato** crosswise into 6 slices.

• Place a burger on the bottom half of each bun. Add 2 slices of bacon, 3 slices of tomato, and a few **basil** leaves. Enjoy.

THAI BASIL BEEF SAUTÉ

Cut of top round beef
1⅓ pounds (600 g)

Thai basil
40 leaves

Garlic
4 cloves

Extra-virgin olive oil
6 tablespoons (90 mL)

Soy sauce
¼ cup (60 mL)

 Salt, pepper

Preparation time: 10 min.

Cooking time: 5 min.

• Cut the **beef** into small pieces; wash the **basil** leaves; peel and chop the **garlic**.

• In a large pan over high heat, sauté the **meat** with the **olive oil** and **garlic** for 3 minutes. Turn off heat. Mix in the **soy sauce** and **basil leaves**. Season with salt and pepper.

GREEK STUFFED EGGPLANT

Eggplant
x 2 (large)

Ground beef
12 ounces (350 g)

Feta cheese
3½ ounces (100 g)

Dried oregano
1 tablespoon (5 g)

Light cream
¼ cup (60 mL)

Extra-virgin olive oil
¼ cup (60 mL)

**Preparation time:
10 min.
Cooking time: 40 min.**

• Preheat the oven to 350°F/180°C. Wrap the **eggplants** individually in aluminum foil and bake for 25 minutes. Finely crumble the **feta**. Cut the eggplants in half, remove the flesh, and mix it with the **beef**, feta, and **oregano**. Stuff the mixture into the eggplant skins.

• Arrange them in a baking dish, drizzle with the **cream** and **olive oil,** and bake for 15 minutes more. Serve directly from the dish.

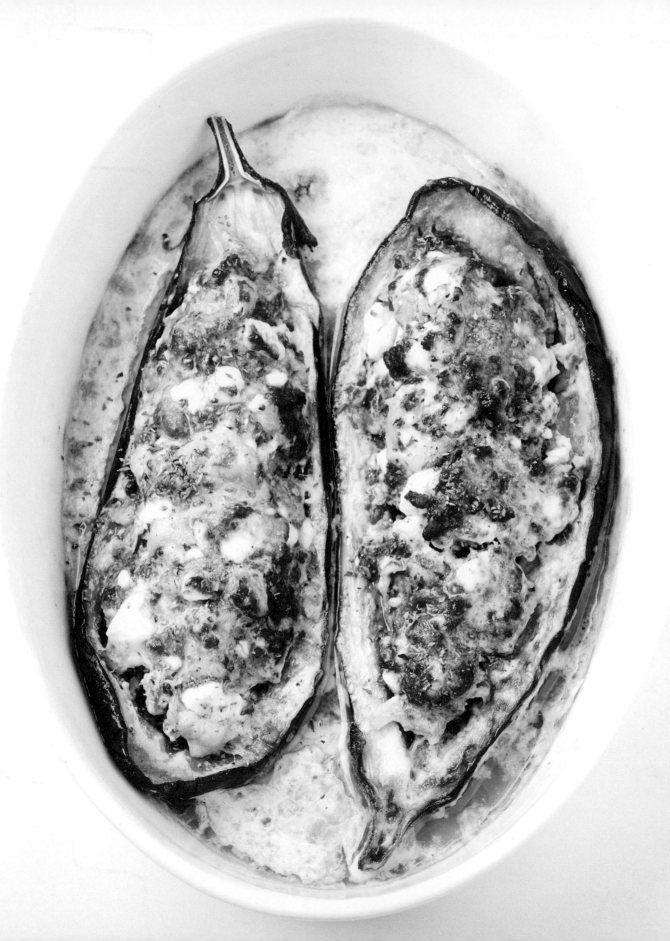

STEAK ROQUEFORT

Thickly cut rump roast steaks
x 4 (about 6 ounces/170 g each)

Roquefort
7 ounces (200 g)

Preparation time: 5 min.
Cooking time: 10 min.

- Cut the **Roquefort** into small pieces.
- In a hot pan, without fat, cook the **steaks** for 3 minutes on each side. Remove from the heat and let sit for 3 minutes. Cover with **Roquefort** and serve.

PORK WITH CHERRIES

Pork loin spareribs
x 4

Cherries
x 24 (pitted)

 **1 tablespoon (15 mL) extra-virgin olive oil**

🧂🧂 **Salt, pepper**

👦👦👦👦

🕐

Preparation time: 15 min.
Cooking time: 35 min.

• Cut the **pork** into cubes. In a hot skillet, sear the **pork** with the **olive oil**. Reduce the heat to medium, and cook for 25 minutes until nicely browned, stirring occasionally.
• Stir in the **cherries** and cook for 10 minutes more. Season with salt and **pepper** and serve.

SOY-MAPLE PORK CHOPS

Pork chops
x 4

Soy sauce
½ cup (120 mL)

Maple syrup
½ cup (120 mL)

Thyme
8 sprigs

Rosemary
2 sprigs

Sage
1 bunch

Salt, pepper

**Preparation time:
10 min., plus 1 hr.
marinating time
Cooking time: 25 min.**

• Put the **pork chops** in a baking dish and add the **herbs**. Mix together the **soy sauce** and **maple syrup** and pour the mixture over the pork. Marinate for 1 hour in the refrigerator. Preheat the oven to 350°F/180°C. Remove and reserve the herbs. Bake the pork chops for 15 minutes, basting them with the cooking juices in the pan. Season with salt and pepper, return the herbs to the dish, and bake for 10 minutes more, basting regularly.

BBQ PORK SPARERIBS

Pork spare ribs
2¾ pounds (1.25 kg)

Ketchup
¼ cup (60 mL)

Soy sauce
¼ cup (60 mL)

Honey
2 tablespoons (40 g)

Thyme
4 sprigs

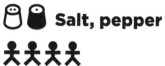 **Salt, pepper**

👥👥👥👥

🕐

**Preparation time:
10 min.
Cooking time: 50 min.**

• Combine the **ketchup**, **soy sauce**, **honey**, and **thyme**. Set aside.
• Preheat the oven to 325°F/170°C. Cut the **spareribs** into large chunks. Bake for 30 minutes. Remove, drain the fat off, and put them back in the pan. Brush with the sauce and put them back in the oven for 20 minutes more, glazing regularly to keep them moist. Season with salt and pepper and enjoy.

PINEAPPLE PORK

Pork chops
x 4

Vegetable oil
¼ cup (60 mL)

Soy sauce
6 tablespoons (90 mL)

Canned pineapple
4 slices
6 tablespoons juice (90 mL)

Cilantro
1 bunch

**Preparation time:
10 min.
Cooking time: 25 min.**

• Heat the **oil** in a skillet over medium-high heat. Cook the **pork chops** for 15 minutes. Cut the **pineapple rings** into pieces and add them to the skillet along with the **pineapple juice** and **soy sauce**.

• Cook over low heat, basting the pork regularly with the pan juices, for 10 minutes, until lightly golden. Arrange the pork chops on a plate, top with the pan sauce, and snip the **cilantro** over the top with scissors. Enjoy.

PORK SPARERIBS WITH TOMATOES AND OLIVES

Pork spareribs
3⅓ pounds (1.5 kg)

Crushed tomatoes
1 can (28 ounces or 800 g)

Black olives, pitted, marinated à la grecque
5 ounces (150 g)

Rosemary
4 sprigs

 Salt, pepper

👤👤👤👤

🕐

Preparation time: 10 min.
Cooking time: 2 hrs.

• Separate the **spareribs** and place them in a cast-iron casserole dish. Add the **tomatoes**, **olives**, half the **rosemary**, and 13½ fluid ounces (400 mL) water.
• Cover and cook over very low heat for 2 hours. Add a little water during the cooking if the sauce reduces too much. Add the remaining rosemary, season with salt and pepper, and enjoy.

CARAMEL PORK LOIN

Pork loin
1¾ pounds (800 g)

Honey
6 tablespoons (120 g)

Soy sauce
6 tablespoons (90 mL)

Sesame seeds
1 tablespoon (10 g)

👤👤👤👤

🕐

Preparation time: 5 min.
Cooking time:
1 hr., 30 min.

• Preheat the oven to 325°F/170°C. Bake the **pork loin** for 1 hour. Drain the fat off and add the **honey** and **soy sauce**.
• Bake for 30 minutes more, glazing regularly with sauce to keep it moist. Sprinkle with **sesame seeds**. Cut it into small pieces, top with **honey-soy** sauce and enjoy with rice, if desired.

MEDALLIONS OF PORK WITH BEER AND APPLES

Medallions of pork
2 pounds (900 g)

Beer
1½ cups (480 mL)

Apples
x 4

Cumin
1 tablespoon (5 g)

Extra-virgin olive oil
2 tablespoons (30 mL)

 Salt, pepper

👥👥👥👥

🕐

**Preparation time:
15 min.**

**Cooking time:
1hr. 30 min.**

- Heat the **olive oil** in a cast-iron casserole dish over high heat. Brown the **pork**, then pour in the **beer**. Reduce the heat to low and simmer, covered, for 1 hour.
- Peel, core, and dice the **apples** and add them to the casserole dish. Cook for 30 minutes more. Add the **cumin**, season with salt and pepper, and serve directly from the casserole dish.

PORK ROAST WITH BELL PEPPERS

Assorted bell peppers
2 pounds (1 kg)

Garlic
8 cloves

Extra-virgin olive oil
¼ cup (60 mL)

Pork roast
2¾ pounds (1.25 kg)

Thyme
4 sprigs

Balsamic vinegar
¼ cup (60 mL)

Salt, pepper

Preparation time: 8 min.
Cooking time: 45 min.

• Stem and seed the **peppers** and cut them into thin slices. Crush the **garlic**, leaving its skin on.

• In a large saucepan over medium-high heat, heat the **olive oil**. Sauté the **pork** for 10 minutes. Add the **bell peppers**, **garlic**, and **thyme**. Season with salt and pepper. Cover, reduce the heat to medium and cook for 45 minutes. Mix in the **vinegar** and enjoy.

STUFFED CABBAGE

Savoy cabbage
8 leaves

Ground sausage
7 ounces (200 g)

Ground veal
7 ounces (200 g)

Raisins
⅓ cup (50 g)

Egg
x 1

Extra-virgin olive oil
2 tablespoons (30 mL)

 Salt, pepper

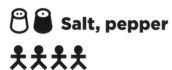

**Preparation time:
20 min.
Cooking time: 40 min.**

• Preheat the oven to 325°F/170°C. Toss the **cabbage** leaves into boiling water for 2 minutes. Remove and cool. Remove the tough parts and cut the leaves into two.

• Mix the **sausage**, **veal**, **raisins**, and **egg**. Season with salt and pepper. Lay out the cabbage and divide the meat mixture among them. Roll them up and place in a baking pan. Drizzle with **olive oil** and bake for 35 minutes.

ENDIVE WITH PROSCIUTTO

Heavy (whipping) cream
1 cup (240 ml)

Grated mozzarella cheese
9 ounces (255 g)

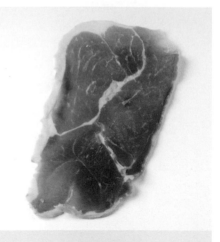

Prosciutto
4 thin slices

Endive
x 4

🧂 **Pepper**

👨👨👨👨

🕐

**Preparation time:
10 min.
Cooking time: 25 min.**

• Preheat the oven to 350°F/180°C. Mix the **cream** and **cheese**. Cut the **endives** and **prosciutto** in half lengthwise. Wrap each **endive** half in a one-half slice of **prosciutto** and place in a baking dish.

• Cover with the sauce, season with pepper, and bake for 25 minutes or until golden brown.

MEDITERRANEAN MEATBALLS

Ground beef
7 ounces (200 g)

Ground sausage
7 ounces (200 g)

Cumin
2 tablespoons (5 g)

Egg
x 1

Assorted bell peppers
x 3

Extra-virgin olive oil
2 tablespoons (30 mL)

Salt, pepper

**Preparation time:
10 min.
Cooking time: 35 min.**

• Preheat the oven to 325°F/170°C. Knead together the **beef**, **sausage**, **cumin**, and **egg**. Shape the mixture into uniformly sized balls.

• Cut the **bell peppers** into strips. Arrange everything in a baking dish and drizzle with **olive oil**. Season with salt and pepper. Bake for 35 minutes.

• Add 2 tablespoons (30 mL) of water to the pan, mixing it into a sauce.

MERGUEZ SAUSAGE WITH CHERRY TOMATOES

Rosemary
2 sprigs

Cherry tomatoes
1 pound (455 g), assorted

Merguez sausage links
x 4

Salt, pepper

**Preparation time:
10 min.
Cooking time: 20 min.**

• Preheat the oven to 325°F/170°C. Wash and chop the **rosemary**. Cut the **tomatoes** in half. Prick the **merguez sausages** with a fork and place them in a baking dish. Bake for 10 minutes.

• Add the **tomatoes** and cook for 10 minutes more. Sprinkle with **rosemary**, season with salt and pepper, and mix. Enjoy with mashed potatoes, if desired.

MAPLE SESAME CHICKEN WINGS

Chicken wings
x 20

Maple syrup
3½ tablespoons (50 mL)

Sesame seeds
¼ cup (40 g)

Sesame oil
2 tablespoons (30 mL)

Salt, pepper

**Preparation time:
10 min.
Cooking time: 35 min.**

• Preheat the oven to 350°F/180°C. Place **wings** on a large rimmed baking sheet and bake for 20 minutes. Add the **maple syrup** and bake for 15 minutes more to brown the chicken, stirring at regular intervals.

• Sprinkle with the **sesame seeds**. Season with salt and pepper, drizzle with the **sesame oil**, and enjoy.

CITRUS CHICKEN DRUMSTICKS

Chicken drumsticks
x 8

Limes
x 3

Oranges
x 3

Honey
6 tablespoons (90 mL)

Thyme
6 sprigs

 **Salt, pepper**

👤👤👤👤

🕐

**Preparation time:
10 min.
Cooking time: 35 min.**

• Preheat the oven to 350°F/180°C. Place the **drumsticks** on a large rimmed baking sheet and bake for 20 minutes, until the drumsticks have begun to brown.

• Slice the **limes** and **oranges** and add them to the baking sheet. Add the **honey** and **thyme**. Bake for 15 minutes more, stirring at regular intervals. Season with salt and pepper, and enjoy.

CHICKEN LEGS WITH SAGE BUTTER

Chicken legs
x 4

Sage
1 bunch

Butter
½ cup (1 stick or 110 g)

  Salt, pepper

🕐

**Preparation time:
10 min.
Cooking time: 45 min.
Standing time: 5 min.**

• Preheat the oven to 350°F/180°C. Bake the **chicken legs** for 40 minutes, basting regularly with the cooking juices. Season with salt and pepper.

• Wash the **sage** and remove the leaves, cutting large ones in half.

• Cook the **butter** with the **sage** over high heat until golden, about 5 minutes. Pour the **sage butter** over the **chicken**. Let stand for 5 minutes before serving.

CHICKEN WITH CASHEWS

Chicken breast
x 4, boneless, skinless

White onion
x 1

Cashews
7 ounces (200 g)

Honey
2 tablespoons (40 g)

Soy sauce
¼ cup (60 mL)

Cilantro
1 bunch

🕴🕴🕴🕴

🫙 **3 tablespoons (45 mL) extra-virgin olive oil**

🕐
**Preparation time: 5 min.
Cooking time: 15 min.**

• Wash and chop the **cilantro**; set aside. Cut the **chicken** into bite-size pieces. In a skillet over medium-high heat, heat the **olive oil**. Sauté the **chicken** for about 5 minutes. Add the chopped **onion** and **cashews**. Brown for 5 minutes more.
• Pour in the **honey** and **soy sauce**. Cook for an additional 5 minutes, stirring. Add the **cilantro** and serve.

CHICKEN LEGS WITH LEMONGRASS AND COCONUT

Chicken legs
x 4

Tomatoes
x 4

Preserved lemons
x 4

Lemongrass
2 stalks

Basil
20 leaves

Coconut milk
14 fluid ounces (420 mL)

 **Salt, pepper**

**Preparation time:
15 min.
Cooking time: 1 hr.**

• Preheat the oven to 325°F/170°C. Cut the **chicken legs** in half and place them in a large baking dish. Thinly slice the **lemongrass**; chop the **tomatoes** and **preserved lemons**. Add them all to the dish, along with the **basil** and **coconut milk**. Season with salt and pepper.

• Bake for 1 hour, basting occasionally. Once the **chicken** is nicely cooked, serve in the pan and enjoy with rice, if desired.

CHICKEN FINGERS WITH CREAMED AVOCADO

Avocados
x 2

Basil
10 leaves

Lemons
x 2

Chicken breasts
x 4, boneless, skinless

Eggs
x 2

Bread crumbs
9 ounces (255 g)

Salt, pepper
+ sauté pan with
2 inches of frying oil

Preparation time:
15 min.
Cooking time: 5 min.

• Heat the oil in the skillet over medium-high heat. Peel the **avocado**. Scoop out the flesh and mix with the **basil** and the juice of the **lemons**. Season with salt and pepper.

• Beat the **eggs**. Cut the **chicken** into thin strips. Dip them into the eggs and then into the **bread crumbs**. Fry for 5 minutes. Enjoy with the creamed avocado.

CHICKEN BREASTS WITH PROSCIUTTO

Chicken breasts
x 4

Prosciutto
4 slices Tomatoes

Tomatoes
x 4 large

Thyme
4 sprigs

Bay leaves
4

Extra-virgin olive oil
¼ cup (120 mL)

 Pepper

**Preparation time:
15 min.
Cooking time: 40 min.**

• Preheat the oven to 350°F/180°C. Cut each **chicken** breast and **prosciutto slice** into 6 slices and wrap the pieces with the prosciutto. Thickly slice the **tomatoes** and arrange them at the bottom of a gratin dish.

• Add the chicken, **thyme**, **bay leaves**, and **olive oil**. Season with pepper and bake for 40 minutes. Serve directly from the gratin dish.

ROAST CHICKEN WITH PAPRIKA

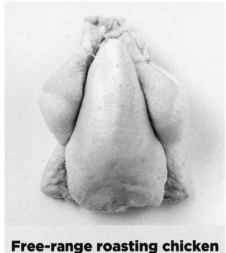

Free-range roasting chicken
x 1

Paprika
1 tablespoon (5 g)

Curry powder
2 teaspoons

Lemons
x 2

Extra-virgin olive oil
¼ cup (60 mL)

 Salt, pepper

👤👤👤👤

🕐

Preparation time: 5 min.
Cooking time: 40 min.

• Preheat the oven to 350°F/180°C. Season the **chicken** with salt and pepper. Combine the **paprika**, **curry**, juice of the **lemons**, and **olive oil**. Brush over the **chicken**.
• Bake for 40 minutes, basting regularly. Arrange the cooked **chicken** on a plate and enjoy with its cooking juices.

LIME AND GINGER COLA CHICKEN

Chicken thighs
x 4

Extra-virgin olive oil
2 tablespoons (30 mL)

Cola
1 can (12 ounces or 330 mL)

Fresh ginger
1¾ ounces (50 g)

Limes
x 2

**Preparation time:
10 min.
Cooking time: 50 min.**

• Halve the **chicken thighs**. Peel and grate the **ginger**. Zest and juice the **limes**. Heat the **olive oil** over high heat in a heavy-based casserole dish. Sear the chicken until nicely browned, then add the ginger, **cola**, and lime zest and juice.
• Reduce the heat to low and cook for 45 minutes, basting with the pan juices from time to time. Serve directly from the casserole dish.

PEANUT CHICKEN SAUTÉ

Chicken breasts
x 4

Soy sauce
6 tablespoons (90 mL)

Peanut butter
3 tablespoons (45 mL)

Iceberg lettuce
x 1

Toasted peanuts
⅓ cup (50 g)

 **2 tablespoons (30 mL) peanut oil**

Preparation time: 10 min.
Cooking time: 25 min.

• Cut the **chicken** into bite-size pieces. Heat the **oil** in a skillet over medium-high heat. Add the chicken and cook for 15 minutes. Add the **soy sauce** and **peanut butter**. Reduce the heat to medium and cook, stirring, for 10 minutes.

• Thinly slice the **lettuce** and arrange it in a serving dish. Arrange the warm chicken on top. Crush the **peanuts**, sprinkle them over the top, and enjoy.

CHICKEN TAGINE

Chicken thighs
x 4

Extra-virgin olive oil
2 tablespoons (30 mL)

Zucchini
x 4 medium

Preserved lemons
x 1

Honey
¼ cup (60 mL)

Saffron
10 threads

 Salt, pepper

**Preparation time:
20 min.
Cooking time: 45 min.**

• Heat the **olive oil** in a heavy-bottomed casserole dish over medium-high heat. Halve the **chicken thighs** and brown them for 20 minutes. Slice the **zucchini** and **lemons** crosswise (discarding any seeds from the lemons) and add them to the casserole.

• Add the **honey** and **saffron**, reduce the heat to low, and cook, stirring occasionally, for 25 minutes. Add a little water if the pan looks dry or the honey browns. Season with salt and pepper, and serve directly from the casserole dish.

SAUTÉED CHICKEN WITH PORCINI AND CHESTNUTS

Dried porcini mushrooms
⅓ ounce (10 g)

Chicken breasts
x 4, boneless, skinless

Light cream
2½ cups (600 mL)

Chestnuts
14 ounces (400 g), bottled

Extra-virgin olive oil
3 tablespoons (45 mL)

Salt, pepper + pan with oil

👤👤👤👤

Preparation time: 15 min.
Cooking time: 35 min.

• Soak the **porcini** in 5 fluid ounces (150 mL) of water. Cut the **chicken breasts** into pieces. In a large saucepan over medium-high heat, sauté the **chicken** with the oil, about 5 minutes. Squeeze the excess water out of the **porcini**, chop, and add them, with their water, to the pan.

• Boil for 5 minutes to reduce. Add the **cream** and **chestnuts**. Reduce the heat to low and simmer for 25 minutes. Season with salt and pepper and enjoy.

PARSLEY PARMESAN CHICKEN

Chicken legs
x 4

Extra-virgin olive oil
2 tablespoons (30 mL)

Flat-leaf parsley
1 bunch

Organic lemons
x 4

Grated Parmesan cheese
¼ cup (25 g)

 **Salt, pepper**

👤👤👤👤

🕐

Preparation time: 8 min.
Cooking time: 45 min.

• Preheat the oven to 350°F/180°C. Bake the **chicken legs** for 40 minutes. Season with salt and pepper. Drizzle with **olive oil**.

• Wash and chop the **parsley**. Zest and juice the **lemons**, straining out any seeds. Mix the lemon zest and juice with the **Parmesan**. Sprinkle over the **chicken** and cook for 5 minutes more.

TARRAGON CHICKEN

Tarragon
6 sprigs

Chicken breasts
x 4

Paprika
4 tablespoons (28 g)

Light cream
1 fluid ounce (30 mL)

Extra-virgin olive oil
2 tablespoons (30 mL)

**Salt, pepper
+ pan plus oil**

**Preparation time: 5 min.
Cooking time: 12 min.**

- Wash the **tarragon** and remove the leaves.
- In a large pan over medium high heat, heat the oil. Cut up the **chicken breasts**. Sauté them in the oil for about 5 minutes. Stir in the **paprika** and **cream**.
- Reduce the heat to medium and cook for 10 minutes, stirring. Mix in the **tarragon** and season with salt and pepper.

CHICKEN THIGHS WITH FRENCH MUSTARD

Chicken thighs
x 4

Light cream
¾ cup (360 mL)

French mustard
¼ cup (120 mL)

Grated Swiss cheese
4 ounces (120 g)

Thyme
8 sprigs

**Preparation time:
10 min.
Cooking time: 45 min.**

• Preheat the oven to 325°F/170°C. Halve the **chicken thighs** and arrange them in a single layer in a baking dish. Mix the **cream**, **mustard**, and **cheese** and pour the mixture over the chicken. Bake for 45 minutes. Pick the leaves off the **thyme** and scatter them over the chicken. Enjoy.

CHICKEN COLOMBO

Chicken legs
x 4

Onions
x 2 (large)

Cilantro
1 bunch

Coconut milk
16 fluid ounces (480 mL)

Vindaloo curry paste
4 tablespoons (60 g)

Salt, pepper

👤👤👤👤

🕐

**Preparation time:
15 min.
Cooking time: 45 min.**

• Preheat the oven to 325°F/170°C. Cut the **chicken legs** in half and peel and chop the **onion**. Combine them in a large baking dish. Add the **cilantro**, **coconut milk**, and **curry paste**. Season with salt and pepper.
• Bake for 45 minutes, basting occasionally. Serve immediately in the pan and enjoy with rice, if desired.

TURKEY AND VEGETABLE STIR-FRY WITH PEANUTS

Turkey breast
x 4

Zucchini
x 1

Red bell pepper
x 1

Soy sauce
6 tablespoons (90 mL)

Toasted peanuts
⅓ cup (50 g)

Basil
1 bunch

2 tablespoons (30 mL) extra-virgin olive oil

🧍🧍🧍🧍

Preparation time: 10 min.
Cooking time: 20 min.

• Slice the **turkey breasts** into strips. Slice the **zucchini** and **bell pepper** into short sticks. Crush the **peanuts**. Cut the **basil** into fine strips with scissors.

• Heat the **olive oil** in a skillet or wok over high heat. Sear the turkey and vegetables, stirring occasionally, for 10 minutes. Add the **soy sauce** and peanuts. Cook for 10 minutes more. Add the basil, mix, and enjoy.

POTATOES WITH DUCK CONFIT

Potatoes
1⅓ pounds (600 g), large

Duck confit
4 legs

Tapenade
2 tablespoons (30 g)

Thyme
4 sprigs

 Salt, pepper

🕐
**Preparation time:
10 min.
Cooking time: 45 min.**

• Preheat the oven to 350°F/180°C. Peel and thinly slice the **potatoes**. Bone the **duck**, chop the skin and meat, and mix together the meat, skin, **tapenade**, and **thyme**.

• In a baking dish, alternate layers of **duck** and **potatoes**. Bake for 45 minutes. When the potatoes are golden, serve with a side salad, if desired.

ROSEMARY DUCK BREAST WITH APRICOTS

Duck breasts
x 2

Rosemary
4 sprigs

Apricots
x 12 (firm)

Honey
2 tablespoons (40 g)

Soy sauce
½ cup (120 mL)

Preparation time: 8 min.
Cooking time: 11 min.
Resting time: 3 min.

• Preheat the oven to 350°F/180°C. Cut **apricots** and remove the pit. Place the **duck** breasts in a nonstick baking dish and bake for 6 minutes. Flip and discard the fat. Add the **rosemary**, **apricots**, **honey**, and **soy sauce**. Return to the oven for 5 minutes more. Remove and let stand for 3 minutes.
• Slice the **duck** breasts and serve with the **apricots** and sauce.

DUCK BREAST WITH TURNIPS AND RADISHES

Tarragon
1 bunch

Baby turnips
x 12 (small)

Pink radishes
x 12

Extra-virgin olive oil
2 tablespoons (30 mL)

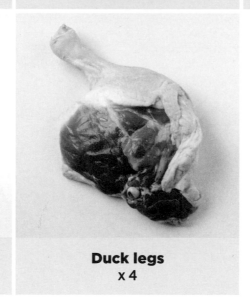

Duck legs
x 4

Salt, pepper

**Preparation time:
10 min.
Cooking time:
1 hr., 5 min.**

- Wash the **tarragon** and remove the leaves. Wash, peel, and trim the **turnips** and **radishes**.
- In a Dutch oven over medium-high heat, heat the **olive oil**. Brown the **duck legs** for 5 minutes. Add the **turnips** and **radishes**. Pour 1¼ cups (300 mL) of water into the pan.
- Cover and cook for 1 hour over low heat. Add the **tarragon**. Season with salt and pepper. Mix and serve.

DUCK CONFIT PARMENTIER

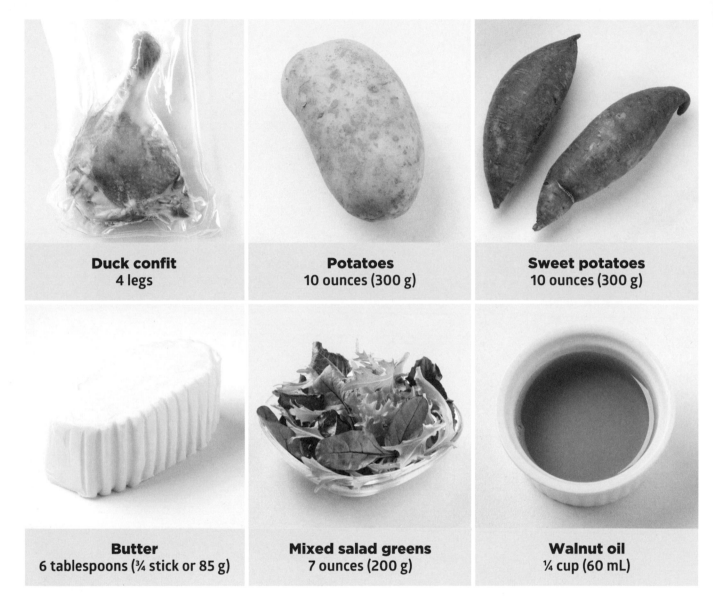

Duck confit
4 legs

Potatoes
10 ounces (300 g)

Sweet potatoes
10 ounces (300 g)

Butter
6 tablespoons (¾ stick or 85 g)

Mixed salad greens
7 ounces (200 g)

Walnut oil
¼ cup (60 mL)

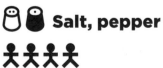 **Salt, pepper**

👤👤👤👤

🕐

**Preparation time:
15 min.
Cooking time: 1 hr.**

• Preheat the oven to 325°F/170°C. Bake the **duck** for 30 minutes. Peel the **potatoes** and **sweet potatoes**. Cook them in lightly salted water for about 30 minutes, or until soft. Drain, add the **butter**, and mash with a fork. Season with salt and pepper.

• Bone the **duck**. Chop the **duck** meat with its skin. Dress the **salad** with the **walnut oil**. Plate the mashed **potatoes**. Top with the **duck** and finish with the **salad** on top.

TURKEY LEG WITH SCALLION SAUCE

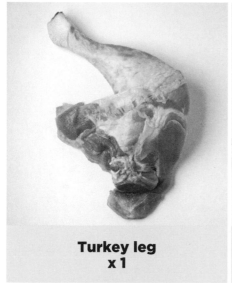

Turkey leg
x 1

Scallions
1 bunch

Maple syrup
6 tablespoons (120 g)

Soy sauce
¼ cup (60 mL)

Preparation time:
10 min.
Cooking time: 1 hr.

• Preheat the oven to 350°F/180°C. Place the **turkey leg** in a baking dish and bake for 30 minutes.

• Peel and thinly slice the **scallions** with their stems on and arrange them around the **turkey**. Top with the **maple syrup** and **soy sauce**.

• Cook for 30 minutes more, basting the turkey in its cooking liquid. Serve with fresh pasta, if desired.

RABBIT IN MUSTARD SAUCE

Dijon mustard
4 tablespoons (40 g)

Heavy (whipping) cream
7 fluid ounces (200 mL)

Fresh thyme leaves
2 tablespoons (5 g)

Rabbit legs
x 4

Garlic
8 cloves

Extra-virgin olive oil
2 tablespoons (30 mL)

 Salt, pepper

Preparation time: 5 min.
Cooking time: 45 min.

• Preheat the oven to 350°F/180°C. Whisk the **mustard** with the **cream** and **thyme**.

• Place the **rabbit legs** and the **garlic** cloves in their skins into a large baking dish.

• Season with salt and pepper and drizzle with **olive oil**. Bake for 20 minutes.

• Pour on the **mustard cream** and bake for 25 minutes more.

SOLE FILLETS WITH PESTO

Sole fillets
x 8

Pesto
8 tablespoons (120 g)

 **Salt, pepper**

👤👤👤👤

🕑

Preparation time: 5 min.
Cooking time: 35 min.

• Preheat the oven to 325°F/170°C. Brush the **sole fillets** with the **pesto**, roll them up, and place them in a baking dish.
• Bake for 35 minutes. Enjoy immediately with mashed potatoes or fresh pasta, if desired.

TARRAGON SKATE TERRINE

Tarragon
1 bunch

Skate wing (whole with skin)
2 pounds (1.2 kg)

**Preparation time:
10 min.
Cooking time: 20 min.
Chilling time: overnight**

• Wash and chop the **tarragon**. Place the **skate** in a heavy-bottomed pot over low heat. Add enough water to cover and cook for 20 minutes. Drain, reserving ¼ cup (5 centiliters) of cooking water.

• Remove and discard the skin and bones. Mix the **skate** flesh with the **tarragon** and reserved cooking water.

• Tightly pack the fish in the terrine, cover, and refrigerate overnight. Serve thick slices plain or with oil and vinegar dressing, if desired.

SEA BASS WITH RASPBERRIES AND TARRAGON

Tarragon
4 sprigs

Raspberries
x 20

Sea bass
1 pound (455 g), boneless, skinless

Lemons
x 2

Extra-virgin olive oil
¼ cup (60 mL)

🧂🫙 **Salt, pepper**

👥👥👥👥

🕐
**Preparation time:
10 min.**

• Wash and chop the **tarragon**. Crush the **raspberries**. Juice the **lemons**, straining out any seeds. Cut the **sea bass** into thin slices and arrange on 4 small plates.

• Top with the **raspberries**, **tarragon**, **lemon** juice, and **olive oil**. Season with salt and pepper and enjoy with toast, if desired.

COD FILLETS WITH TOMATO AND BASIL

Garlic
2 cloves

Tomatoes
x 4 (average-size)

Basil
1 bunch

Extra-virgin olive oil
¼ cup (60 mL)

Cod fillets
x 4 (fresh or frozen)

 **Salt, pepper**

**Preparation time:
10 min.
Cooking time: 20 min.**

• Preheat the oven to 325°F/170°C. Peel the **garlic**. Dice the **tomatoes**. Wash the **basil** and remove the leaves. Mix them all in a food processor with 2 tablespoons (30 mL) of **olive oil**. Season with salt and pepper and set aside. Place the **cod fillets** in a baking dish and drizzle with the remaining 2 tablespoons (30 mL) of **olive oil**. Bake for 20 minutes.

• Top the fish with **tomato-basil** sauce and enjoy.

SEA BREAM IN CRUSTY SALT AND HERBS

Rosemary
4 large sprigs

Thyme
10 sprigs

Flat-leaf parsley
½ bunch

Coarse salt
1⅓ pounds (600 g)

Sea bream
x 1 (3⅓ pounds or 1.5 kg), gutted

**Preparation time:
10 min.
Cooking time: 30 min.**

- Preheat the oven to 325°F/170°C. Wash the **herbs** and remove the leaves. Mix them with the **salt**.
- Place the **sea bream** on a rimmed baking sheet. Cover it with a thick layer of the herbed **salt**. Bake for 30 minutes.
- Break the **salt** crust, remove the skin, and pull out the fillets. Enjoy with a little olive oil, if desired.

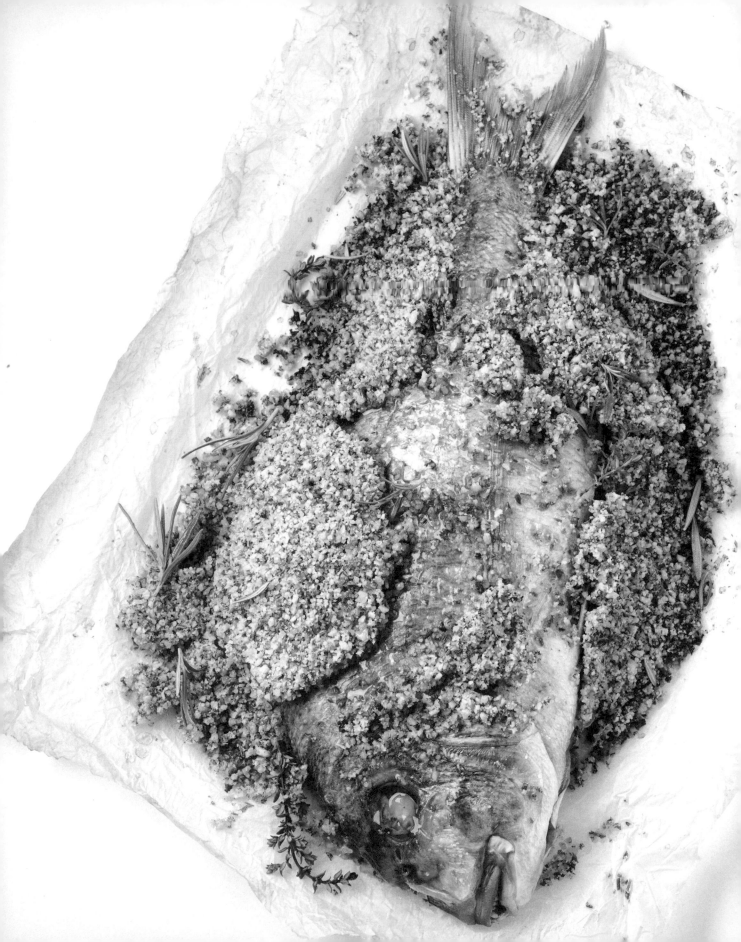

THAI LEMONGRASS SEA BREAM

Tomatoes
x 4

Lemongrass
2 stalks

Extra-virgin olive oil
¼ cup (60 mL)

Coconut milk
1 cup (240 mL)

Sea bream fillets
x 4 (skin on)

 **Salt, pepper**

**Preparation time:
10 min.
Cooking time: 40 min.**

- Preheat the oven to 350°F/180°C. Dice the **tomatoes** and cut the **lemongrass** into thin strips.
- Place the **tomatoes**, **lemongrass**, **olive oil**, and **coconut milk** in a baking dish. Bake for 30 minutes, stirring occasionally.
- Add the **sea bream fillets** with their skins. Season with salt and pepper. Return to the oven for 10 minutes more. Serve immediately in the dish.

SEA BASS TARTARE WITH MANGO

Mango
x1

Sea bass fillets
x 8 (boneless, skinless)

Cilantro
1 bunch

Coconut milk
2 tablespoons (30 mL)

Extra-virgin olive oil
¼ cup (60 mL)

Lemon
x 1 (2 tablespoons [30 mL] juice)

Salt, pepper

**Preparation time:
10 min.**

• Peel and cut the **mango** into cubes. Wash and chop the **cilantro**. Cut the **sea bass** into cubes.
• Mix the **sea bass**, **mango**, **cilantro**, **coconut milk**, **olive oil**, and **lemon juice**. Season with salt and pepper. Enjoy chilled with toast, if desired.

CIDER MONKFISH WITH PROSCIUTTO

Button mushrooms
10 ounces (300 g)

Monkfish
1¾ pounds (800 g), cleaned

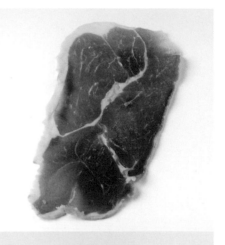

Prosciutto
4 thin slices

Butter
¼ cup (½ stick or 55 g)

Apple cider
1 cup (240 mL)

Light cream
1 cup (240 mL)

 Salt, pepper

🕐

**Preparation time:
15 min.
Cooking time: 30 min.**

• Wash and thinly slice the **mushrooms**. Wrap the **monkfish** with the **prosciutto** and secure with kitchen string.

• In a large saucepan over high heat, melt the **butter**. Sauté the **monkfish** and **mushrooms**, about 3 minutes, browning. Transfer the **monkfish** to a plate.

• Pour in the **cider**. Simmer until reduced to three-fourths. Add the **cream**. Cook for 5 minutes over high heat. Add the **monkfish**; cover and cook for 20 minutes more. Season with salt and pepper.

MONKFISH WITH PORCINI

Dried porcini
1½ ounces (40 g)

Monkfish cheeks
x 12

Butter
¼ cup (½ stick or 55 g)

Soy sauce
2 tablespoons (30 mL)

Light cream
2 cups (480 mL)

Hazelnut oil
2 tablespoons (30 mL)

 Salt, pepper

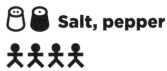

Soaking time: 30 min.
Preparation time: 5 min.
Cooking time: 25 min.

• Soak the **porcini** for 30 minutes in 1¼ cups (300 mL) of water. Drain and cut into pieces, reserving the soaking liquid. Simmer the liquid until reduced by half.

• In a large saucepan over medium-high heat, sauté the **monkfish** with the **butter** for 5 minutes. Add the soaking liquid and **soy sauce**. Simmer until reduced by half. Add the **cream** and the **porcini**. Cook for 10 minutes more over low heat. Serve drizzled with **hazelnut oil**.

MACKEREL WITH MUSTARD AND THYME

Mackerel fillets
x 4, boneless, skin on

Dijon mustard
4 tablespoons (44 g)

Fresh thyme leaves
1 tablespoon (2 g)

 Salt, pepper

👤👤👤👤

🕐

Preparation time: 5 min.
Cooking time: 25 min.

• Preheat the oven to 325°F/170°C. Place the **mackerel** in a baking dish. Coat it with **mustard**. Season with salt and pepper and sprinkle with **thyme**.

• Bake for 25 minutes, or until the **mackerel** are nicely cooked and crisp.

RED MULLET WITH MANDARIN JUICE

Mandarin oranges
x 8

Soy sauce
2 tablespoons (30 mL)

Extra-virgin olive oil
¼ cup (60 mL)

Red mullet fillets
x 8 (fresh or frozen)

 **Salt, pepper**

👤👤👤👤

🕐

**Preparation time:
10 min.
Cooking time: 5 min.**

- Preheat the oven to 350°F/180°C. Squeeze the juice from the **mandarins** and mix it with the **soy sauce** and **olive oil**.
- Place the **red mullet fillets** in a baking dish and bake for 5 minutes. Transfer to a shallow serving dish and top with the **mandarin** juice mixture.

BAKED SWORDFISH WITH TOMATO

Tomatoes
x 2

Swordfish fillets
1 pound (455 g)

Extra-virgin olive oil
¼ cup (60 mL)

White wine
3 tablespoons plus 1 teaspoon
(50 mL)

Fresh thyme leaves
1 tablespoon (2 g)

Bay leaves
x 2

 Salt, pepper

**Preparation time:
10 min.
Cooking time: 30 min.**

• Preheat the oven to 325°F/170°C. Wash and slice the **tomatoes**. Cut the **swordfish fillets** into pieces.
• Arrange the **tomatoes** and **fish** in a baking dish in alternating layers. Season with salt and pepper. Add the **olive oil**, **white wine**, **thyme**, and **bay leaves**. Bake for 30 minutes. Enjoy piping hot with rice, if desired.

HADDOCK AND ZUCCHINI GRATIN

Zucchini
x 3

Haddock
14 ounces (400 g)

Basil
20 leaves

Roughly grated Parmesan cheese
7 ounces (200 g)

Extra-virgin olive oil
¼ cup (60 mL)

 **Salt, pepper**

**Preparation time:
10 min.
Cooking time: 35 min.**

• Preheat the oven to 325°F/170°C. Wash and trim the **zucchini**. With a vegetable peeler, thinly slice it lengthwise. Cut the **haddock** into thin slices. Wash and chop the **basil**.
• Layer the **zucchini**, **Parmesan**, **haddock**, **basil**, and **olive oil** in a baking dish. Bake for 35 minutes and enjoy.

CURED SALMON WITH ANISE

Salmon fillets
1⅓ pounds (600 g), boneless, skinless

Coarse salt
2 tablespoons (35 g)

Sugar
2 cuil. à soupe

Dill
1 bunch

Aniseed
2 tablespoons (13.4 g)

Extra-virgin olive oil
2 tablespoons (30 mL)

 **Salt, pepper**

👤👤👤👤

🕐

**Preparation time:
10 min.
Cooking time: 12 min.**

• Place the **salmon** in a container, cover with the **salt**, **sugar**, and three-fourths of the **dill**. Cover the container with plastic wrap and leave to cure in the refrigerator for 12 hours.
• Drain the **salmon** and cut into thin slices. Top with the remaining **dill**, chopped, the **aniseed**, and **olive oil**.

CURRIED MINT SALMON

Zucchini
x 2

Cherry tomatoes
10½ ounces (300 g)

Curry powder
2 tablespoons (10 g)

Coconut milk
1½ cups (360 mL)

Salmon steaks
1⅓ pounds (600 g)

Mint
20 leaves

Salt, pepper

2 tablespoons (30 mL) extra-virgin olive oil

👤👤👤👤

🕐

Preparation time: 15 min.
Cooking time: 25 min.

• Finely chop the **zucchini**. Chop the **tomatoes**. Dice the **salmon**. Heat the **oil** in a wok or skillet over medium-high heat. Sauté the zucchini and tomatoes for 10 minutes. Add the **curry powder** and **coconut milk** and cook over very low heat for 10 minutes. Add the salmon and cook for 5 minutes more.

• Season with salt and pepper, and allow to cool. Snip the **mint** over the top with scissors, mix, and enjoy.

SALMON TARTARE WITH ASPARAGUS

Green asparagus
x 8

Salmon fillets
1 pound (455 g), boneless, skinless

Lemons
x 3

Extra-virgin olive oil
¼ cup (60 mL)

  Salt, pepper

**Preparation time:
10 min.
Cooking time: 1 min.
Resting time: 5 min.**

- Wash the **asparagus** and remove the tough woody ends. Dip them into boiling water for 1 minute. Remove, cool, and cut into small pieces.
- Cut the **salmon** into small cubes and mix with the **asparagus**. Squeeze the **lemons** over and drizzle with **olive oil**. Season with salt and pepper. Refrigerate for 5 minutes. Enjoy with toast, if desired.

BAKED JOHN DORY WITH LEMON SAUCE

Cilantro
1 bunch

Preserved lemons
x 2

Extra-virgin olive oil
6 tablespoons (90 mL)

Pomegranate seeds
1¾ ounces (50 g)

Soy sauce
2 tablespoons (30 mL)

John Dory
x 1 (3½ pounds or 1.6 kg), cleaned

 Pepper

👤👤👤👤

🕐

**Preparation time:
10 min.
Cooking time: 25 min.**

• Preheat the oven to 325°F/170°C. Wash and chop the **cilantro**. Peel the **preserved lemons** and chop the peel. Mix the **cilantro** and **lemon** with the **olive oil** and **soy sauce**. Set aside.

• Place the **John Dory** in a large baking dish. Bake for 25 minutes. Season with pepper and enjoy the hot fish topped with **lemon** sauce, with a salad on the side, if desired.

TUNA CARPACCIO WITH CILANTRO

Cilantro
1 bunch

Extra-virgin olive oil
¼ cup (60 mL)

Soy sauce
2 tablespoons (30 mL)

Lime
x 1

Tuna or bonito
1 pound (455 g)

 Pepper

**Preparation time:
10 min.**

- Wash the **cilantro** and remove the leaves. Mix the **olive oil** with the **soy sauce** and the juice of the **lime**.
- Cut the **tuna** into thin slices and arrange on 4 plates. Keep refrigerated.
- Before serving, divide the sauce among the plates, sprinkle with **cilantro**, season with pepper, and enjoy with toast, if desired.

TUNA WITH RED BELL PEPPERS

Red bell peppers
x 2

Green bell pepper
x 1

Tuna in oil
2 cans (5 ounces or 140 g each)

🧂🧂 **Salt, pepper**

🧍🧍🧍🧍

🕐

Preparation time:
10 min.

Cooking time: 25 min.

• Wash, stem, and seed the **peppers** and then thinly slice. Place the **peppers** in a large saucepan with the **tuna oil**. Simmer for 25 minutes over low heat.

• Turn off the heat and add the **tuna**. Season with salt and pepper. Mix, then enjoy with fresh pasta, if desired.

RAW TUNA IN SESAME OIL

Tuna
1 pound (455 g), red or white

Limes
x 2

Sesame oil
3 tablespoons (45 mL)

Sesame seeds
1 tablespoon (10 g)

Soy sauce
6 tablespoons (90 mL)

**Preparation time:
10 min.
Cooking time: 10 min.**

• Dice the **tuna** and mix with the juice of the **limes**, the **sesame oil**, **sesame seeds**, and **soy sauce**. Marinate in the refrigerator for 10 minutes, stirring occasionally.
• Enjoy with toasted farmhouse bread, if desired.

CURRY BASIL TUNA SALAD

Tuna in oil
1 can (5 ounces or 140 g)

Curry powder
1 tablespoon (5 g)

Ricotta cheese
5 ounces (150 g)

Basil
1 bunch

Salt, pepper

**Preparation time:
10 min.**

• Using a fork, mix the **tuna**, half the oil from the can, the **curry powder**, and the **ricotta**. Season with salt and pepper.

• Snip the **basil** over the top with scissors. Mix and serve on toasted bread or with sticks of raw vegetables, if desired.

SWORDFISH KEBABS WITH SAFFRON

Swordfish steaks
4 steaks (160 g each)

Green bell peppers
x 2

Extra-virgin olive oil
6 tablespoons (90 mL)

Dried oregano
1 tablespoon (5 g)

Saffron
1 large pinch of saffron threads

 **Salt, pepper**

**Preparation time:
20 min., plus 1 hr.
marinating time
Cooking time: 10 min.**

• Put the **swordfish** in a baking dish. Cut the **bell peppers** into bite-size pieces and add them to the dish. Pour over the **olive oil**, sprinkle with the **oregano** and **saffron**, and toss to coat. Marinate the swordfish for 1 hour. Preheat the oven to 350°F/180°C. Thread alternating pieces of fish and bell pepper on wooden skewers and set them on a rimmed baking sheet.

• Bake for 10 minutes, and then arrange them on a serving platter. Drizzle with the oil from the marinade. Season with salt and pepper, and enjoy.

SQUID FRICASSÉE WITH BASIL

Garlic
2 cloves

Extra-virgin olive oil
¼ cup (60 mL)

Squid
1¾ pounds (800 g), spiny portions removed

White wine
1 glass (5 fluid ounces or 150 mL)

Crushed tomatoes
1 can (14 ounces or 400 g)

Basil
20 leaves

Salt, pepper

**Preparation time:
10 min.
Cooking time: 45 min.**

• Peel and chop the **garlic**. Heat the **olive oil** in a saucepan over medium-high heat. Sauté the **squid** with the **garlic** for 5 minutes, allowing it to brown. Pour in the **white wine**. Simmer to reduce by half, then add the **tomatoes**.

• Season with salt and pepper. Cover and simmer for 40 minutes over a low heat. Add the **basil leaves** and mix before serving.

OCTOPUS BAKE

Red onions
x 2

Extra-virgin olive oil
¼ cup (60 mL)

Octopus
2¾ pounds (1.25 kg)

Red wine
1 bottle (25 fluid ounces
or 750 mL)

Tomato purée
1 can (28 ounces or 800 g)

Thyme
4 sprigs

Salt, pepper

**Preparation time:
10 min.
Cooking time: 1 hr.**

• Peel and thinly slice the **onions**. Cut the **octopus** into small pieces.

• In a skillet over medium-high heat, heat the **olive oil**. Sauté the **onions** and **octopus** for 5 minutes. Pour in the **wine**. Add the **tomato purée** and **thyme**. Cover and simmer for 1 hour over low heat, stirring occasionally. Enjoy piping hot accompanied by fresh pasta, if desired.

JAMBALAYA

Rice
1¾ cups (360 g)

Chorizo
x 4

Cooked shrimp
x 16 (jumbo)

Red bell peppers
x 2

Onions
x 2

Paprika
2 teaspoons

 **Salt, pepper**

4 teaspoons (20 mL) extra-virgin olive oil

Preparation time: 15 min.
Cooking time: 40 min.

• Bring 3½ cups (840 mL) lightly salted water to a boil in a medium saucepan. Add the **rice** and cook as directed on the package.

• Slice the **sausages** crosswise. Shell the **shrimp**. Thinly slice the **bell peppers** and **onions**. Heat the **olive oil** in a large skillet over medium-high heat. Cook the sausages, bell peppers, and onions for 20 minutes. Add the rice, shrimp, and **paprika** and stir. Cook, stirring regularly, for 20 minutes more. Season with salt and pepper, and enjoy.

SHRIMP CEVICHE WITH LIME

Limes
x 4

Cilantro
1 bunch

Prawns
x 8 (jumbo)

Extra-virgin olive oil
6 tablespoons (90 mL)

 **Salt, pepper**

**Preparation time:
15 min.**
Cooking time: 15 min.

• Juice the **limes**. Wash the **cilantro**, remove the leaves, and chop them. Shell the **prawns**.

• In the refrigerator, marinate the **shrimp** in a dish with the **olive oil**, **lime** juice, and **cilantro** for 15 minutes. Season with and salt and pepper and enjoy with slices of toast, if desired.

JUMBO SHRIMP CURRY

Shrimp
x 8 (jumbo)

Extra-virgin olive oil
2 tablespoons (30 mL)

Basil
40 leaves

Coconut milk
32 fluid ounces (1 L)

Curry powder
2 tablespoons (10 g)

 Salt, pepper

👤👤👤👤

🕐

**Preparation time:
15 min.**

Cooking time: 20 min.

• Preheat the oven to 350°F/180°C. Shell the bodies of the **shrimp**, keeping the heads and tails on, and place them in a baking dish.

• Add the **olive oil**, **basil**, and the **coconut milk** mixed with the **curry powder**. Season with salt and pepper. Bake for 20 minutes.

• Serve immediately from the pan and enjoy with rice or fresh pasta, if desired.

SHRIMP WITH VANILLA BUTTER

Vanilla beans
x 4

Softened butter
4¼ ounces (120 g)

Shrimp
x 8 (jumbo)

 Salt, pepper

👥👥👥👥

🕐

Preparation time: 8 min.
Cooking time: 10 min.

- Split the **vanilla beans**. Scrape out the seeds and mix them with the **butter**. Reserve the beans.
- Cut the **shrimp** in half. Sauté it in the **butter** over medium-high heat for 2 to 3 minutes. Add the **vanilla beans** and cook for 6 to 8 minutes over low heat.
- Season with salt and pepper and enjoy with mashed potatoes, if desired.

LOBSTERS WITH CREAM

Lobsters
x 2 (1¾ pounds or 800 g each)

Butter
6 tablespoons (¾ stick or 85 g)

Cognac
3 tablespoons plus 1 teaspoon
(50 mL)

Light cream
16 fluid ounces (480 mL)

Tomato paste
2 tablespoons (30 g)

 Salt, pepper

Preparation time: 5 min.
Cooking time: 35 min.
Resting time: 30 min.

- Plunge the **lobsters** into boiling water for 1 minute.
- In a large saucepan over medium-high heat, heat the **butter**. Sauté the **lobsters** for 5 to 7 minutes in the hot **butter**.
- Remove the lobsters to a clean platter. Deglaze the pan with the **Cognac**, then add the **cream** and **tomato paste**. Whisk to combine. Replace the lobster, cover, and cook for 20 minutes over low heat. Remove from the heat and let sit, covered, for 30 minutes to steep the flavors. Reheat before serving.

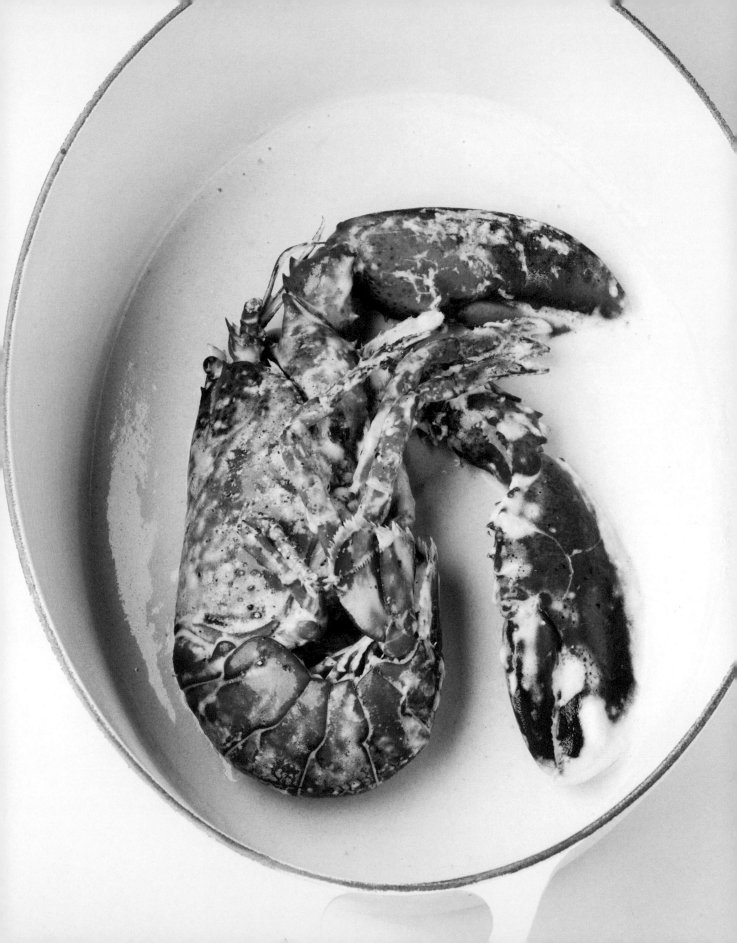

HOT OYSTERS WITH GINGER

Oysters
x 8 (large)

Heavy (whipping) cream
1 tablespoon (15 mL)

Butter
6 tablespoons (¾ stick or 85 g)

Fresh ginger
1 ounce (30 g), grated

Lime
x 1

Salmon roe
2 tablespoons (30 g)

Salt, pepper

Preparation time:
20 min.
Cooking time: 5 min.

• Open the **oysters** and pour their water into a small saucepan. Shell and poach them for 2 seconds in their water. Drain and replace them in their shells.

• In a separate saucepan over medium heat, heat the **cream**. Add the **butter** in pieces. Remove from the heat and whisk. Add the **ginger**, the juice of the **lime**, and the **salmon roe**. Coat the **oysters** in the sauce.

OYSTERS, POMEGRANATE, AND CILANTRO

Pomegranate
x 1

Cilantro
1 bunch

Limes
x 3

Soy sauce
6 tablespoons (90 mL)

Extra-virgin olive oil
¼ cup (60 mL)

Oysters
x 24, shucked

**Preparation time:
20 min.**

• Peel the **pomegranate** and remove the seeds. Wash and chop the **cilantro**. Juice the **limes**. Mix all these ingredients in a large bowl.

• Arrange the **oysters** on 4 individual plates. Cover with the marinade. Allow to stand for 3 minutes and enjoy.

MUSSELS MARINIÈRE WITH CURRY

Mussels
2 quarts (2 liters)

Heavy (whipping) cream
1½ cups (360 mL)

Thyme
4 sprigs

Curry powder
1 tablespoon (5 g)

Salt, pepper

👤👤👤👤

🕐

**Preparation time:
10 min.
Cooking time: 5 min.**

• Scrape and wash the **mussels**. Put them into a large saucepan with the **cream**, **thyme**, and **curry powder**. Bring to a boil and cook for 5 minutes over high heat while stirring.

• Once the **mussels** open, remove from the heat. Season with salt and pepper and enjoy. Discard any unopened mussels.

CLAMS WITH COCONUT MILK

Lemongrass
2 stalks

Coconut milk
16 fluid ounces (480 mL)

Thyme
2 sprigs

Clams
x 24

🧂🧂 **Salt, pepper**

👤👤👤👤

⏲

Preparation time:
10 min.
Cooking time: 10 min.

- Peel and thinly slice the **lemongrass**.
- Add the **coconut milk**, **lemongrass**, **thyme**, and **clams** to a saucepan. Bring to a boil while stirring. When the **clams** open, remove them from heat. Arrange in 4 individual bowls. Discard any unopened clams.

SCALLOP CARPACCIO WITH PASSION FRUIT

Passion fruits
x 3

Extra-virgin olive oil
¼ cup (60 mL)

Scallops
x 12, fresh or frozen (thawed)

  Salt, pepper

👤👤👤👤

🕐

**Preparation time:
10 min.
Cooking time: 5 min.**

- Cut the **passion fruit** in two, scoop out the flesh and juice, and mix with the **olive oil**.
- Cut the **scallops** into fine slices and arrange in a rosette on 4 plates. Brush with the **passion fruit** oil.
- Season with salt and pepper. Marinate for 5 minutes and enjoy.

SCALLOPS AND GAZPACHO WITH HERBS

Basil
20 leaves

Dill
1 bunch

Scallops
x 12, fresh or frozen (thawed)

Extra-virgin olive oil
6 tablespoons (90 mL)

Gazpacho
32 fluid ounces (1 L)

Pepper

👤👤👤👤

🕐
**Preparation time:
15 min.
Cooking time: 2 min.**

• Wash and roughly chop the **basil** and **dill**. In a pan over medium-high heat, brown the **scallops** for 2 minutes in 3 tablespoons (45 mL) of **olive oil**.

• Serve the **gazpacho** in 4 shallow dishes. Add the **scallops** and herbs. Season with pepper, drizzle with the remaining 3 tablespoons (45 mL) of **olive oil**, and enjoy.

CHOCOLATE FLAKES

Milk chocolate
7 ounces (200 g)

Cornflakes
4½ cups (130 g)

**Preparation time:
15 min.
Refrigeration: 1 hr.**

• Melt the **chocolate** in a bain-marie or double boiler. Add the **cornflakes** and mix.
• Shape equal amounts into small heaps and place them on a large baking sheet. Refrigerate for 1 hour to set, and then serve.

NUTELLA BAKE

Eggs
x 4

Nutella®
9 ounces (255 g)

**Preparation time:
10 min.
Cooking time: 5 min.**

- Preheat the oven to 350°F/180°C. In a bowl, beat the **eggs** for 8 minutes with an electric mixer.
- Soften the **Nutella** in a microwave, about 30 seconds. Using a spatula, gently mix it into the beaten eggs. Fill 4 ramekin dishes and bake for 5 minutes. Enjoy hot with a scoop of vanilla ice cream, if desired.

COCONUT DROPS

Egg whites
x 2

Sugar
6 tablespoons (80 g)

Grated coconut
2¼ cups (180 g)

**Preparation time:
10 min.
Cooking time: 5 min.**

• Preheat the oven to 400°F/210°C. With your clean fingertips, mix the **egg whites** with the **sugar** and **coconut**.

• Shape into small heaps and arrange on a parchment paper-lined baking sheet so they don't stick. Bake for 5 minutes. Cool and enjoy.

CHEESECAKE WITH SPECULOOS CRUST

Cream cheese
10½ oz (300 g)

Heavy cream
¾ cup (200 mL)

Eggs
x 2

Limes
x 2

Speculoos cookies
9 ounces (250 g)

Butter
6 tablespoons (¾ stick or 85 g)

**Preparation time:
15 min., plus 1 hr.
chilling time
Cooking time: 40 min.**

• Preheat the oven to 350°F/180°C. Zest and juice the **limes** and transfer to a food processor. Add the **cream cheese**, **cream**, and **eggs** and process until well combined. Refrigerate for 1 hour. Melt the **butter** in a small saucepan. Crush the **speculoos cookies** and mix 7 ounces (200 g) of the cookie crumbs with the melted butter. Line the bottom of a tart dish with the crumb mixture and bake for 10 minutes. Allow to cool. Pour in the cheese mixture and bake for 30 minutes. Allow to cool, sprinkle with the remaining cookie crumbs, and enjoy.

PISTACHIO AND CHERRY COOKIES

Candied cherries
3½ ounces (100 g)

Pistachios
1¾ ounces (50 g), shelled

Butter
½ cup (1 stick or 112 g)

Sugar
¼ cup (50 g)

Flour
¾ cup (100 g)

**Preparation time:
15 min.
Refrigeration time: 1 hr.
Cooking time: 10 min.**

• Chop the **cherries** and **pistachios**. Mix together the **butter**, **sugar**, **flour**, **cherries**, and **pistachios**. Shape the dough into a log and refrigerate for 1 hour.
• Preheat the oven to 350°F/180°C.
• Slice the dough evenly into ½-inch-thick (1 cm) cookies and arrange on a baking sheet. Bake for 10 minutes. Cool before serving.

GRATED APPLE TART

Puff pastry
x 1 sheet

Apples
x 4

Granulated sugar
6 tablespoons (75 g)

Butter
⅓ cup (80 g)

Confectioner's sugar
1 tablespoon (10 g)

**Preparation time:
10 min.
Cooking time: 25 min.**

• Preheat the oven to 350°F/180°C. Cut the **butter** into small pieces. Unroll the **puff pastry** on a baking sheet without removing the parchment paper. Peel and grate the **apples** by hand, then spread them evenly over the pastry, leaving a border around the edges. Turn over the border to form a rim.
• Sprinkle with the **granulated sugar**, dot with the butter, and bake for 25 minutes. Allow to cool, then dust with the **confectioner's sugar** before serving.

CHOCOLATE CREAM PUFFS WITH PASSION FRUIT SORBET

Dark chocolate
7 ounces (200 g)

Heavy (whipping) cream
¾ cup (180 mL)

Pastry puffs
x 12

Passion fruit sorbet
10 ounces (300 g)

👥👥👥👥

🕐
**Preparation time:
15 min.**

• Crush the **chocolate** with a heavy knife and transfer it to a mixing bowl. In a small saucepan set over medium heat, bring the **cream** to a boil. Pour it over the **chocolate** while stirring to melt. Set aside in a bain-marie.

• Fill **pastry puffs** with **sorbet**. Serve on individual plates, top with hot **chocolate**, and enjoy.

PEAR CLAFOUTIS TART

Pie crust pastry
x 1

Eggs
x 3

Sugar
¾ cup (150 g)

Almond flour
6 tablespoons (40 g)

Heavy cream
1 cup (240 mL)

Pears
x 4

**Preparation time:
15 min.
Cooking time: 45 min.**

• Preheat the oven to 325°F/170°C. Peel, core, and dice the **pears**. Line a pie pan with the **pie crust** without removing the parchment paper. Turn the edges toward the inside, pressing with your fingertips.

• Beat the **eggs**, **sugar**, **almond flour**, and **cream** and pour into the pie crust. Add the pear pieces. Bake for 45 minutes. Enjoy warm or cold.

RASPBERRY WHIPPED CREAM

Heavy (whipping) cream
2½ cups (600 mL)

Confectioner's sugar
1 tablespoon (10 g)

Raspberries
14 ounces (400 g)

Preparation time:
10 min.

Refrigeration time:
10 min.

• In a very cold bowl whip the cold **cream** into peaks with an electric mixer. Add the **sugar** and **raspberries**, continuing to whip for 2 minutes more. Spoon into dessert bowls. Refrigerate for 10 minutes and enjoy.

WILD STRAWBERRIES WITH MASCARPONE WHIPPED CREAM

Mascarpone
9 ounces (255 g)

Heavy (whipping) cream
11 fluid ounces (330 mL)

Confectioner's sugar
1 tablespoon (10 g)

Wild strawberries
14 ounces (400 g)

**Preparation time:
10 min.
Refrigeration time: 1 hr.**

• In the large bowl, mix the **mascarpone**, **cream**, and **sugar** with an electric mixer. Refrigerate for 1 hour. Five minutes before serving, whip the mixture until smooth.
• Serve layered in glasses with **wild strawberries**.

CHOCOLATE CAKE

Butter
⅔ cup (150 g)

Sugar
6 tablespoons (80 g)

Chocolate
7 ounces (200 g)

Flour
6 tablespoons (50 g)

Eggs
x 4

**Preparation time:
20 min.
Cooking time: 35 min.**

• Preheat the oven to 350°F/180°C. Chop the **butter** into small pieces and roughly mix it into the **sugar**. Chop the **chocolate**, melt it in a bain-marie, and fold it into the butter-sugar mixture. Separate the **eggs**. Add the egg yolks to the chocolate mixture one at a time while stirring. Mix in the **flour**. Beat the egg whites until they hold firm peaks, then fold them into the batter.

• Pour the batter into a buttered loaf pan and bake for 35 minutes. Allow to cool slightly, then turn the cake out of the pan. Enjoy warm or cold.

CINNAMON AND LADY APPLE PASTRIES

Lady apples
x 4

Butter
¼ cup (½ stick or 55 g)

Cinnamon
2 tablespoons (14 g)

Puff pastry
x 1 sheet

Sugar
¼ cup (50 g)

**Preparation time:
10 min.
Cooking time: 30 min.**

- Peel and dice the **apples**. In a pan over medium heat, sauté them for 5 minutes with **butter** and **cinnamon**. Cool.
- Preheat the oven to 350°F/180°C. Roll out the **puff pastry** on a baking sheet, cover half with the **apples**, fold the other half of the pastry over the apples, and sprinkle with the **sugar**. Bake for 25 minutes. Enjoy hot or cold.

STRAWBERRIES IN WINE SYRUP WITH MINT

Red wine
7 fluid ounces (200 mL)

Sugar cubes
x 15

Star anise
x 3

Cinnamon
2 sticks

Mint
1 bunch

Strawberries
2 pints (1½ pounds or 680 g)

**Preparation time:
10 min.**
Cooking time: 25 min.
Steeping time: 3 hr.

- Wash the **mint**. Wash, hull, and slice the **strawberries**.
- Combine the **wine**, **sugar**, and **spices** in a saucepan. Cook over low heat for 25 minutes. Turn off the heat under the syrup. Add the **mint**, cover, and steep for 3 hours in a cool place.
- Remove the **mint**, add the **strawberries**, and enjoy.

WATERMELON WITH LEMON SYRUP

Organic lemons
x 2

Confectioner's sugar
2 tablespoons (20 g)

Watermelon
2 pounds (900 g)

👤👤👤👤

🕐

**Preparation time:
10 min.
Cooking time: 25 min.**

• Zest the **lemons** and squeeze their juice into a saucepan, straining out any seeds. Add 3 tablespoons plus 1 teaspoon [50 mL]) of water and the **sugar**. Cook over low heat, letting the flavors infuse, for 25 minutes. Cool.

• Remove the **watermelon** rind and cut the flesh into cubes. Mix the **watermelon** with the **lemon** syrup. Chill and enjoy.

STRAWBERRY SALAD WITH BASIL

Strawberries
14 ounces (400 g)

Confectioner's sugar
1 tablespoon (10 g)

Lemons
x 2

Basil
10 leaves

Extra-virgin olive oil
2 tablespoons (30 mL)

**Preparation time:
10 min.**

**Refrigeration time:
15 min.**

Cooking time: 25 min.

• Wash and finely chop the **basil**. Set aside. Juice the **lemons**, straining out any seeds. Wash, hull, and slice the **strawberries** and place them in a mixing bowl. Toss with the **sugar** and **lemon** juice.

• Refrigerate for 15 minutes to infuse the flavors. Add the **basil** and **olive oil**. Mix and enjoy.

380

COCOA AND BLUEBERRY CREAM

Heavy (whipping) cream
2½ cups (600 mL)

Dark cocoa powder
2 tablespoons (10 g)

Confectioner's sugar
2 teaspoons

Blueberries
14 ounces (400 g)

Refrigeration time: 1 hr.
Preparation time: 15 min.

- Pour the **cream** into a mixing bowl and refrigerate for 1 hour. Five minutes before serving, beat the **cream** until stiff peaks are formed. Add the **cocoa** and **sugar**. Beat for an additional minute to mix well.
- Serve in ramekins with the **blueberries**.

INDEX

Black Dog & Leventhal Publishers
Hachette Book Group
1290 Avenue of the Americas
New York, NY 10104

www.hachettebookgroup.com
www.blackdogandleventhal.com

Originally published in 2015 by Hachette Livre in France.

First English Edition: September 2016

Black Dog & Leventhal Publishers is an imprint of Hachette Books, a division of Hachette Book Group. The Black Dog & Leventhal Publishers name and logo are trademarks of Hachette Book Group, Inc.

The publisher is not responsible for websites (or their content) that are not owned by the publisher.

The Hachette Speakers Bureau provides a wide range of authors for speaking events. To find out more, go to www.HachetteSpeakersBureau.com or call (866) 376-6591.

Print book interior design by Marie-Paule Jaulme.

Library of Congress Control Number: 2016941523

ISBN: 978-0-316-31772-6

Printed in China

IM

10 9 8 7 6 5 4